Keto Diet Book FOR BEGINNERS UK

The Complete Beginners Keto Diet Cookbook

ISBN: 9798557168007

TABLE OF CONTENTS

Introduction

What Is the Keto Diet? 8

How does Keto Diet work? 9

What types of meals should you eat on Keto Diet? 10

What food can you eat on Keto Diet? 10

What food can't you eat on Keto Diet? 10

What foods should you limit on Keto Diet? 11

Benefits of keto diet? 11

How much does Keto Diet cost? 11

Is the Keto Diet Healthy? 12

Will Keto Diet help you lose weight? 12

Can Keto Diet prevent or control diabetes? 13

Is Keto Diet nutritious? 13

Is Keto Diet a heart-healthy diet? 13

Does Keto Diet have any health risks? 14

Does Keto Diet allow for restrictions and preferences? 14

How much should you exercise on Keto Diet? 15

Getting the Right Balance Is Tricky 15

How easy is Keto Diet to follow? 16

Things to remember 16

Recipe Notes 16

THE 35 DAY MEAL PLAN

First Week Meal Plan 18

Second Week Meal Plan 19

Third Week Meal Plan 20

Fourth Week Meal Plan 21

Fifth Week Meal Plan.. 21

Breakfast recipes

Keto oatmeal 23

Keto green smoothie 24

Charismatic Crepes 24

Almond butter muffins 25

Blueberry Whirl Mousse 26

Shrimp Scampi Spinach Salad 26

Strawberry & Blueberry Yogurt Ice-cream 27

Pumpkin Pie Custard 28

Perfect Breakfast Pumpkin Bread 29

PEANUT BUTTER MUFFINS 30

Cheesy Frittata Muffins 30

Cheesy Scrambled Eggs 31

Almond Lemon Cake Sandwiches 32

Breakfast tacos 33

Classic western omelet 34

CHEDDAR SCRAMBLED EGGS 35

Inside Out Bacon Burger 35

QUICK KETO SCRAMBLE 36

Bacon & Mozzarella Meatballs.. 37

BROWNIE MUFFINS 37

Bacon Infused Sugar Snap Peas.. 38

BREAKFAST BURGERS 39

Mushroom Soup with Fried egg 40

SAUSAGE AND EGG SCRAMBLE 41

Avocado Egg & salami sandwiches.. 42

CREPES WITH BLUEBERRIES 42

Crispy chai waffles 43

Lunch recipes

Tantalizingly Tasty Tomato 44

Buffalo chicken strips 45

Bacon cheddar explosion 46

Eggs with Asparagus 47

Cheddar chorizo meatballs 48

Cheesy scrambled eggs 49

Cheesy spinach 49

Greek Wedge 50

Cheesy Spinach 51

Chicken roulade 51

Cloud Nine BLT 52

Buffalo chicken strip slider 53

Bacon, cheddar & chive mug biscuit 54

Pure Perfection Pepperoni Pizza 55

Cinnamon & orange beef stew 56

Intense Cauliflower Cheese Bake 57

Coffee & red wine beef stew 58

Crispy curry rubbed chicken thigh 59

Greek Salad 60

Drunken five spice beef 60

Overnight Oats 61

Cheesy Frittata Muffins 62

Fried queso fresco 63

Strawberry Cashew Milk 63

Lemon rosemary chicken 64

Keto szechuan chicken 65

Egg & Mackerel Breakfast Kick-Start 66

Omnivore burger with creamed 67

Bacon wrapped pork tenderloin 68

Keto-Classic Cereal 69

Red pepper spinach salad 70

The Magnificent Mushroom 70

Keto Crunchy Cauliflower Hash Browns 71

Baked Egg Breakfast Banquet 72

Classy Cheese & Onion Omelette 72

Dinner recipes

Shredded Fennel Salad with Chicken 73

Roasted pecan green beans 74

Shrimp & cauliflower curry 75

Paleo Lamb Meatballs 76

Simple lunch salad 77

Carob Avocado Mousse 77

Chicken and bacon sausage stir fry 78

Taco tartlets 79

Egg & Bacon Sandwich 80

Thai peanut chicken 81

Vegetable medley 82

Keto-Buzz Blueberry Pancakes 83

Bacon Infused Sugar Snap Peas 84

Inside Out Bacon Burger 85

Mozzarella Pockets of Pleasure 86

What Waffle! 87

Bacon & Egg Pick-me-up 88

No-Fuss Egg Medley Muffins 88

Charming Cream Cheese Breakfast Pancakes 89

Keto Chocolate Hazelnut Muffins 90

Keto Bacon Mini Frittata 91

Bacon and Avocado Caesar Salad 92

Bonus recipes

Vanilla latte cookies 93

Lemon Pepper Tuna Salad 94

Bbq pulled chicken 95

Quick Ground Beef Stir-Fry 96

Pan-Fried Tuscan Chicken "Pasta" 97

Bulletproof coffee 98

Chai spice mug cake 98

Garlic Shrimp Caesar Salad 99

Grilled Ribeyes with Greek Relish 100

Chicken Salad 101

Crunchy Chocolate Coconut Curls 102

Not your caveman's chili 103

Keto snickerdoodle cookies 104

Low carb spice cakes 105

CONCLUSION: **107**

Introduction

The keto diet leverages the body's innate ability to burn fat to fuel activity and weight loss by drastically cutting carbohydrates and increasing the ratio of good fats in the diet. "The keto diet has been used to treat drug-resistant epilepsy for the past 100 years, But it has increasingly been used as a weight-loss diet. It takes advantage of our body's ability to tap into fat stores, like fasting does. This low-carb, high-fat diet is meant to induce ketosis by adjusting macronutrients," or fat, carbs and protein.

Keto diets force the body to use fat as its primary source of energy, an approach that revolves around a biochemical process called ketosis. Ketosis is when your body breaks down both dietary and stored fat for fuel and creates ketones in the process. Ketones are a byproduct of burning fat that are generated in the liver that a can be measured in the blood. If you're going to be strict about the keto diet, you'll likely be testing your blood regularly to track the level of ketones to make sure you're in the target zone for fat burning.

The keto diet was initially developed in the 1920s as a means of treating severe epilepsy in children. This diet was composed of 90% fat, 6% protein and 4% carbohydrates, which helped to quell epileptic seizures. The diet is still used today in people for whom other treatments haven't been successful.

Though classic keto cuts out almost all carbs, there are other, modified versions of the diet that some people use today. Liz Weinandy, a registered dietitian with the Ohio State University Wexner Medical Center, says that the "modified keto diet is 82% fat, 12% protein and 6% carbs. It's very similar to a classic keto diet," but is slightly less extreme in its reliance on fat as the primary source of calories and thus may be marginally easier to stick with longer term.

In either the classic or modified keto approach, the high-fat/very-low-carb ratios can be challenging for most people to achieve in day-to-day life, and as such it may be better to use short-term to cut weight quickly or to cycle in and out of from time to time rather than being a lifestyle approach.

What Is the Keto Diet?

The ketogenic diet is just the opposite. It requires at least 70% of daily calories come from fat, only 5% to 10% from carbohydrates and about 25 percent from protein. On this diet, the body goes into a state of ketosis, where fat is burned for fuel instead of carbohydrate. The diet originated as a treatment for certain severe cases of epilepsy; for unknown reasons, ketosis reduces the occurrence and severity of these seizures.

Over the past few years, the keto diet has been promoted as a weight-loss tool for others. And the anecdotal evidence suggests that, in the short term, it can result in quick and significant weight loss. It may have other short-term benefits as well. A 2012 meta-analysis in the journal Obesity Reviews concluded that a low-carb diet did have "favorable effects" on major cardiovascular risk factors like body weight, blood pressure, cholesterol levels and blood sugar levels. However, "the effects on long-term health are unknown.

How does Keto Diet work?

You can stay on the keto diet indefinitely, do it as a weight-loss plan over a single short period or cycle in and out. Fat-rich foods are key, protein is moderate and carbs are the bad guys. Vogel offers some tips for getting started on keto:

- Educating yourself about carbs and getting familiar with good fats is the first step.
- Before jumping in, experiment with low-carb veggies in the grocery store's natural produce section, find sources of grass-fed meat and learn about hidden sources of sugar, like the coleslaw at your local eatery.
- Don't assume sugar cravings will disappear right away. Instead, stock up on keto-friendly desserts like dark chocolate with nut butter.
- During the first week of carb withdrawal, you might experience symptoms including muscle aches, headaches, fatigue and mental fogginess – and yes, hunger. For early cravings, try nibbling on a high-fat snack such as a bacon strip or some cucumber with avocado mayo.

As the diet moves into the second and third weeks, you'll begin to feel better. Soon, low-carb, high-fat eating will seem more natural as it becomes a habit. By week four, you can expect weight loss, especially if you've been physically active while sticking closely to the plan.

Selecting the right food will be easier as you become accustomed to the keto approach. Instead of lean meats, you'll focus on skin-on poultry, fattier parts like chicken thighs, rib-eye steaks, grass-fed ground beef, fattier fish like salmon, beef brisket or pork shoulder, and bacon. Leafy greens such as spinach, kale and lettuce, along with broccoli, cauliflower and cucumbers, make healthy vegetable choices (but you'll avoid starchy root foods like carrots, potatoes, turnips and parsnips). You can work in less-familiar veggies such as kohlrabi or daikon.

Oils like avocado, olive, canola, flaxseed and palm, as well as mayonnaise will flavor salads while fattening them up. Clarified butter, or ghee, is a fat you'll use for cooking or as a spread.

Start your day with a nut butter-boosted latte, coffee or tea, or have bacon and eggs as a breakfast staple. Stick with whole-fat milk, cheese and other whole dairy products. Use stevia to replace sugar and artificial sweeteners.

In "Keto in 28," author Michelle Hogan details her four-week plan. In the book's menus, carbs are kept to low levels, ranging from 15 to 20 net carbs a day. Net carbs are the total amount of carbohydrates in a serving subtracted by the amount of fiber.

On the other hand, fat makes up a whopping 70 to 73% of the daily diet. Protein rounds out the meal plans, comprising a moderate one-fifth to one-quarter of breakfasts, lunches and dinners daily, along with one or two recommended snacks. (Carb/fat/protein proportions vary from diet to diet with each author.)

For maintenance over time, Vogel suggests taking a cyclical approach and going in and out of ketosis, especially for women.

Dieters use a number of signs to know they're in ketosis, some more subjective than others. Simple DIY urine or blood test results, bad or fruity breath, reduced hunger, sharper mental focus, changes in exercise performance, and weight loss can all indicate ketosis.

What types of meals should you eat on Keto Diet?

If you crave fat, you're in luck. Start your day with a double "rocket fuel" latte, if you like – and don't skimp on the cacao butter. Lunch on ground turkey patties with side of a slaw, or a couple of sausage links. Keto is one diet where you're encouraged to bypass leaner ground beef and also dig into fatty chicken thighs instead of skinless breasts.

Prefer to go meatless? That's entirely possible, especially if you concentrate on low-carb veggies. Slather on some mayo for a tasty fat boost. As you become more comfortable, you may find yourself experimenting with exotic vegetable choices like kohlrabi. If you're including fish-based meals, fattier fish like salmon will help meet keto requirements for moderate protein as well as high fat.

What food can you eat on Keto Diet?

Fatty animal protein
Meat, bacon, eggs, poultry with skin and fish

Oils and natural fats
Olive, canola and palm oil, and cacao butter latte

Vegetables
Spinach, kale, lettuce, broccoli and cucumbers

What food can't you eat on Keto Diet?

Alcohol
Not recommended during the ketosis phase

Sugar
This includes artificial sweeteners (use stevia instead).

What foods should you limit on Keto Diet?

Carbohydrates
Bread and pasta

Starchy root veggies
Potatoes, carrots and turnips

Benefits of keto diet?

There is a ton of hype surrounding the ketogenic diet. Some researchers swear that it is the best diet for most people to be on, while others think it is just another fad diet.

To some degree, both sides of the spectrum are right. There isn't one perfect diet for everyone or every condition, regardless of how many people "believe" in it. The ketogenic diet is no exception to this rule.

However, the ketogenic diet also has plenty of solid research backing up its benefits. It is better than most diets at helping people with:

- Epilepsy
- Type 2 Diabetes
- Type 1 Diabetes
- High Blood Pressure
- Alzheimer's disease
- Parkinson's disease
- Chronic Inflammation
- High Blood Sugar Levels
- Heart Disease
- Fatty Liver Disease
- Cancer
- Migraines

Even if you are not at risk from any of these conditions, the ketogenic diet can be helpful for you too. Some of the benefits that most people experience are:

- Better brain function
- A decrease in inflammation
- An increase in energy
- Improved body composition

How much does Keto Diet cost?

Meat – like grass-fed selections – and fresh veggies are more expensive than most processed or fast foods. What you spend on keto-friendly foods will vary with your choices of protein source and quality. You can select less-expensive, leaner cuts of meat and fatten them up with some oil. Buying less-exotic, in-season veggies will help keep you within budget.

Is the Keto Diet Healthy?

For some people, eliminating carbs and sugar may make them feel different. "Because it's so low carb and sugar is eliminated, they may feel better when they go on it," Weinandy says. But for many keto dieters, this initial period of feeling better can disappear quickly, replaced by the keto flu. Though a modified version of the keto diet may be less likely to cause the keto flu. However, if your body transitions into ketosis, you may develop symptoms.

Keto flu is a common side effect of any keto diet that's typically felt in the early stages of transitioning to ketosis. "The keto flu can include lightheadedness, headaches, fatigue, nausea and constipation," Ossa says. It occurs because "when carbohydrates are restricted, the body rapidly losses fluids and sodium."

One way to combat the keto flu, he says, is by "increasing sodium by 1 to 2 grams per day."

Ossa says other health risks associated with switching to a keto diet may include:

- Muscle loss.
- Micronutrient and mineral deficiencies.
- Altering gut microbiota.

Because there have been so few long-term studies into the diet, "we still don't have definite answers" about the long-term effects of following a ketogenic diet, he says.

For individuals with certain conditions, such as liver disease and kidney disease, the ketogenic diet may not be a good choice. Those with diabetes or other metabolic diseases are advised to speak with a doctor and dietitian before adopting a ketogenic diet.

And that's good advice for anyone who's thinking about adopting the keto diet. Ossa says that before he puts any patient on any type of restrictive diet pattern, "I conduct a full nutritional assessment to understand their past and current dietary habits." Talking with a registered dietitian can help you determine which diet is actually the best one for your particular situation and can help you understand what nutrients you need to make sure you're getting enough of on any protocol.

Will Keto Diet help you lose weight?

Recent studies focusing on keto diets suggest some advantages for short-term weight loss. It's still too soon to tell whether people maintain long-term weight loss from ketogenic diets.

In its 2016 report "Healthy Eating Guidelines & Weight Loss Advice," the Public Health Collaboration, a U.K. nonprofit, evaluated evidence on low-carbohydrate, high-fat diets. (The keto diet falls under the LCHF umbrella.) Among 53 randomized clinical trials comparing LCHF diets to calorie-counting, low-fat diets, a majority of studies showed greater weight loss for the keto-type diets, along with more beneficial health outcomes. The collaboration recommends weight-loss guidelines that include a low-carbohydrate, high-fat diet of real (rather than processed) foods as an acceptable, effective and safe approach.

A small Feb. 20, 2017, study looked at the impact of a six-week ketogenic diet on physical fitness and body composition in 42 healthy adults. The study, published in the journal Nutrition & Metabolism, found a mildly negative impact on physical performance in terms of endurance capacity, peak power and faster exhaustion. Overall, researchers concluded, "Our findings lead us to assume that a [ketogenic diet] does not impact physical fitness in a clinically relevant manner that would impair activities of daily living and aerobic training." The "significant" weight loss of about 4.4 pounds, on average, did not affect muscle mass or function.

Can Keto Diet prevent or control diabetes?

Although it's not typically recommended in the U.S. for people who already have diabetes, a keto diet may have a role in preventing Type 2 diabetes. Avoiding obesity and reducing carbs may lower the body's demand for insulin, promote lower blood sugar levels and prevent blood sugar spikes, all of which relate to diabetes risk. The Public Health Collaboration report includes findings from a British researcher, who used an LCHF diet with patients who have Type 2 diabetes, showing "dramatic" health improvements and cost savings on diabetes drugs that were no longer needed.

Is Keto Diet nutritious?

With its combination of unusually high fat plus remarkably low carb content, experts had enough reservations to place the keto diet way down in this category. Experts expressed particular concern for people with liver or kidney conditions, who should avoid it altogether. The jury is still out whether keto offers more potential health risks or benefits for people with heart conditions or diabetes. With the variety of keto versions and food choices, and different methods for cycling in and out of the diet, hormonal and other changes can vary widely.

Here's a breakdown of the nutritional content of a day's meals on the keto diet, along with recommendations from the government's 2015-20 Dietary Guidelines for Americans. Because this diet is highly individualized, your nutritional intake will vary.

Is Keto Diet a heart-healthy diet?

Low-carb diets like keto may have some heart health benefits. A systematic review of randomized controlled trials comparing low-carb and low-fat diets in overweight and obese patients looked at outcomes for nearly 1,800 patients in 17 studies with short-term (less than one year) follow-up. Low-carb diets were associated with significantly greater weight reduction and significantly lower predicted risk of heart disease tied to hardening of the arteries, compared with low-fat diets, according to the study published October 2015 in the journal PLOS One.

Dr. Eric Westman, director of the Duke Lifestyle Medicine Clinic and an expert in low-carb and keto diets, recommends the keto diet for some of his patients with heart disease. That, he says, is because the metabolic syndrome – a cluster of symptoms including high triglycerides and low "good" HDL cholesterol, high blood pressure, and high blood sugar, linked to heart disease and diabetes – is caused by a diet that's high in processed carbs and low in healthy fats. He sees improved triglyceride and HDL levels in patients on the keto diet.

Other heart risk factors like high blood pressure may improve on the keto diet. However, anyone with an existing heart condition who goes on the diet should be monitored by their health care providers.

Does Keto Diet have any health risks?

Keto could pose health risks, particularly for people with certain medical conditions. People with kidney or liver conditions should not attempt a keto diet. Some experts caution that the diet can lead to muscle loss.

The keto diet isn't for everyone: Pregnant or nursing women, underweight people, women with a history of eating disorders or anyone with heart disease who hasn't first consulted a doctor should avoid the diet. Hormonal changes aren't always beneficial, as the diet can have a dramatic effect on insulin and reproductive hormones. The use of the keto diet for people with diabetes is controversial, and some dietitians advise against it. A person with diabetes, especially someone taking insulin, would require careful monitoring.

Keto diets take different paths, and your nutritional mileage may vary. You could incorporate healthy fats such as avocados and nuts as much as possible and focus on whole, unprocessed foods. In that case, the diet might have disease-preventing properties. On the other hand, if you choose to max out on the least-healthy sources of animal fats and protein like nitrate-packed processed meats, the diet could become part of the problem.

Does Keto Diet allow for restrictions and preferences?

Most people can customize the Keto diet according to their needs. Check individual preferences for more information.

Supplement recommended?

A daily vitamin with minerals including potassium and magnesium can fill in potential gaps while following keto.

Vegetarian or Vegan: It's possible to adapt the keto diet for vegetarians or vegans, but it's more challenging.

Gluten-Free: Yes. The keto diet already avoids high-gluten, high-carb foods such as wheat bread, cookies and pasta. Many nut butters, a keto staple, are also gluten-free.

Low-Salt: Keto can lend itself to a low-salt approach, if you avoid processed meats such as sausage and bacon.

Halal: It's up to you to prepare meals within guidelines.

How much should you exercise on Keto Diet?

To get the most benefit from the keto diet, you should stay physically active. You might need to take it easier during the early ketosis period, especially if you feel fatigued or lightheaded. Walking, running, doing aerobics, weightlifting, training with kettlebells or whatever workout you prefer will boost your energy further. You can find books and online resources on how to adapt keto meals or snacks for athletic training.

Getting the Right Balance Is Tricky

Maintaining the right ratio of macronutrients (fat, carbohydrates and protein) is an important part of the ketogenic diet, and Gioffre says you should shoot for a maximum of 50 grams of net carbohydrates per day. To calculate the net carbs, simply subtract the grams of dietary fiber from the total carbs.

Getting enough fiber is important, and it's something that the keto diet doesn't provide enough of, Gioffre says. You need fiber to help move waste through the digestive system, and if you don't get enough, it can cause digestive problems and elevate the risk for several types of cancer. Fiber also confers heart-health benefits.

Gioffre also notes that research has shown that people who vary their diet are healthier. That means not sticking to the keto diet 24-7. "The body loves variety and dietary variation. If you have less than 50 grams net carbs for four or five days, increase it to 150 grams – that will prevent your body from going into a starvation mode where it stores fat." Giving your body a rest a couple day a week can actually make the ketogenic diet much more effective as a means of weight loss.

However, despite its upsides, the diet has some drawbacks. "The exclusion of whole grains, beans, legumes and a broader variety of vegetables and fruits eliminates a wide variety of beneficial nutrients, all of which are included in other healthy eating plans like Mediterranean and vegan/vegetarian diets," Leman says. Many dietitians will tell you any diet that excludes whole groups of foods isn't the healthiest long-term solution.

How easy is Keto Diet to follow?

If you love morning toast, whole-wheat pasta, pizza and sugary desserts, you could struggle on the keto diet. You'll need time to prepare and educate yourself, and the first week won't be much fun.

Things to remember

A healthy diet is not a solution to anything in and of itself; it must be applied as part of a healthy lifestyle in order to see maximum results.

Think of the ketogenic diet as the foundation of your new body. If you want to build something truly special on top of it then design your lifestyle with that goal in mind.

Cutting out junk food goes without saying, as does ditching bad habits such as smoking and drinking. Exercise, too, will take you to heights you never thought was possible.

So, as you explore these delectable dishes and embark on the keto diet, try not to neglect other areas of responsibility.

Let this be the start of something great!

Recipe Notes

We wanted to make it as simple as possible for you to get in the kitchen and rustle up something special, so you will find each recipe laid out in an easy to follow format.

Remember this diet is designed to rekindle your love of food not extinguish it with rules and regulations, so don't be afraid to experiment.

Use the ingredients as general guidelines and follow the instructions as best you can. You may not get everything the perfect first time, every time but that is what makes it yours!

Keep at it for a full 30 days of eating and you will no doubt establish a few firm favourites that you can turn into your speciality dishes over time.

Each recipe ends with a breakdown of key nutritional information including the number of calories and amount of fats, carbohydrates and protein.

Again, this isn't to be obsessed over. Food is something to be enjoyed, so if you are going to keep a note of your intake levels then just make it a general estimate.

Why no pics? This cookbook is full of fun and flavour and doesn't take itself too seriously. The food is entering your mouth, not a modelling contest, and we don't like to encourage unhealthy obsession about presentation. So just cook, experiment, and enjoy.

Once you start loving what you are eating mealtimes will become something to look forward to. Take this as encouragement, go forth and cook to your heart's content!

THE 35 DAY MEAL PLAN

Now, the moment you've been waiting for – the meal plan! In this chapter, you'll find a 28-day meal plan for the standard ketogenic diet, divided into four weeks. Every day you'll follow the plan to eat breakfast, lunch, and dinner, as well as a snack or dessert with a calorie range between 1,800 and 2,000.

One thing I want to mention before you get started is net carbs.

Many people who follow the ketogenic diet prefer to track net carbs rather than total carbs. To calculate net carbs, you simply take the total carb count of the meal and subtract the grams of fiber since fiber cannot be digested. Personally, I prefer to track total carbs like what I have mentioned in my first book, but I have included the grams of fiber and net carbs in these recipes, so you can choose which way to go.

Personally, I prefer more buffer when it comes to the carb count, because I want to reduce the number of obstacles keeping me from ketosis. Many of my readers as well as friends have raised this point and you can be sure quite a few nights or afternoons were spent in heated debate! Okay, it wasn't that serious but suffice it to say that quite a bit of discussion went into this topic. Therefore, I thought it might be better if I gave you a say in this net carb-total carb debate. You get to choose whichever you prefer. In my personal opinion, when you are in the initial stages of trying to enter ketosis, keeping your total carb count in mind is probably one of the better practices you can adopt. A 20 to 50 gram range of carbs would usually work to push the body into a ketogenic state.

After you have gotten keto adapted and the body gets used to burning fat for fuel, you can then start to bring net carbs into the equation.

Keep in mind the calorie range for these meal plans – if you read my first book and calculated your own daily caloric needs, you may need to make some adjustments. If you're trying the ketogenic diet for the first time, however, it may be easiest to just follow the plan as is until you get the hang of it.

The first week of this 28-day meal plan is designed to be incredibly simple in terms of meal prep so you can focus on learning which foods to eat and which to avoid on the ketogenic diet – that's why you'll find more smoothies and soups here than in the following weeks. If you finish the first week and feel like you still need some time making the adjustment to keto, feel free to repeat it before moving on to week two. The meal plans also take into account left-overs and the yields of various recipes, so that you have minimal waste from your efforts in the kitchen. So, without further ado, let's take a look at the meal plans

35-Days Keto Diet Weight Loss Challenge

First Week Meal Plan

DAYS	BREAKFAST	LUNCH	DINNER
Sunday	Keto oatmeal (Page No: 23)	Buffalo chicken strips (Page No: 44)	Egg & Bacon Sandwich (Page No: 78)
Monday	Keto green smoothie (Page No: 23)	Chicken roulade (Page No: 50)	Keto Bacon Mini Frittata (Page No: 88)
Tuesday	Almond butter muffins (Page No: 25)	Buffalo chicken strips (Page No: 44)	Keto Bacon Mini Frittata (Page No: 88)
Wednesday	Keto oatmeal (Page No: 23)	Carob Avocado Mousse (Page No: 75)	Paleo Lamb Meatballs (Page No: 74)
Thursday	Almond butter muffins (Page No: 25)	Chicken roulade (Page No: 50)	Shrimp & cauliflower curry (Page No: 73)
Friday	Keto green smoothie (Page No: 23)	Fried queso fresco (Page No: 61)	Egg & Bacon Sandwich (Page No: 78)
Saturday	Keto oatmeal (Page No: 23)	Carob Avocado Mousse (Page No: 75)	Paleo Lamb Meatballs (Page No: 74)

35-Days Keto Diet Weight Loss Challenge

Second Week Meal Plan

DAYS	BREAKFAST	LUNCH	DINNER
Sunday	Keto green smoothie (Page No: 23)	Chicken roulade (Page No: 50)	Shrimp & cauliflower curry (Page No: 73)
Monday	Peanut butter muffins (Page No: 29)	Chicken roulade (Page No: 50)	Egg & Bacon Sandwich (Page No: 78)
Tuesday	Keto oatmeal (Page No: 23)	Carob Avocado Mousse (Page No: 75)	Egg & Bacon Sandwich (Page No: 78)
Wednesday	Peanut butter muffins (Page No: 29)	Carob Avocado Mousse (Page No: 75)	Simple lunch salad (Page No: 75)
Thursday	Almond butter muffins (Page No: 25)	Buffalo chicken strips (Page No: 44)	Keto Bacon Mini Frittata (Page No: 88)
Friday	Keto oatmeal (Page No: 23)	Buffalo chicken strips (Page No: 44)	Shrimp & cauliflower curry (Page No: 73)
Saturday	Keto oatmeal (Page No: 23)	Chicken roulade (Page No: 50)	Keto Bacon Mini Frittata (Page No: 88)

35-Days Keto Diet Weight Loss Challenge

Third Week Meal Plan

DAYS	BREAKFAST	LUNCH	DINNER
Sunday	Keto green smoothie (Page No: 23)	Buffalo chicken strips (Page No: 44)	Shrimp & cauliflower curry (Page No: 73)
Monday	Peanut butter muffins (Page No: 29)	Buffalo chicken strips (Page No: 44)	Keto Bacon Mini Frittata (Page No: 88)
Tuesday	Keto oatmeal (Page No: 23)	Chicken roulade (Page No: 50)	Keto Bacon Mini Frittata (Page No: 88)
Wednesday	Peanut butter muffins (Page No: 29)	Fried queso fresco (Page No: 61)	Paleo Lamb Meatballs (Page No: 74)
Thursday	Keto oatmeal (Page No: 23)	Carob Avocado Mousse (Page No: 75)	Paleo Lamb Meatballs (Page No: 74)
Friday	Almond butter muffins (Page No: 25)	Chicken roulade (Page No: 50)	Egg & Bacon Sandwich (Page No: 78)
Saturday	Keto green smoothie (Page No: 23)	Carob Avocado Mousse (Page No: 75)	Simple lunch salad (Page No: 75)

35-Days Keto Diet Weight Loss Challenge

Fourth Week Meal Plan

DAYS	BREAKFAST	LUNCH	DINNER
Sunday	Keto oatmeal (Page No: 23)	Chicken roulade (Page No: 50)	Paleo Lamb Meatballs (Page No: 74)
Monday	Keto green smoothie (Page No: 23)	Buffalo chicken strips (Page No: 44)	Paleo Lamb Meatballs (Page No: 74)
Tuesday	Keto oatmeal (Page No: 23)	Buffalo chicken strips (Page No: 44)	Simple lunch salad (Page No: 75)
Wednesday	Almond butter muffins (Page No: 25)	Chicken roulade (Page No: 50)	Shrimp & cauliflower curry (Page No: 73)
Thursday	Keto green smoothie (Page No: 23)	Fried queso fresco (Page No: 61)	Shrimp & cauliflower curry (Page No: 73)
Friday	Peanut butter muffins (Page No: 29)	Eggs with Asparagus (Page No: 46)	Keto Bacon Mini Frittata (Page No: 88)
Saturday	Keto oatmeal (Page No: 23)	Eggs with Asparagus (Page No: 46)	Keto Bacon Mini Frittata (Page No: 88)

35-Days Keto Diet Weight Loss Challenge

Fifth Week Meal Plan

DAYS	BREAKFAST	LUNCH	DINNER
Sunday	Keto oatmeal (Page No: 23)	Buffalo chicken strips (Page No: 44)	Egg & Bacon Sandwich (Page No: 78)
Monday	Keto green smoothie (Page No: 23)	Chicken roulade (Page No: 50)	Keto Bacon Mini Frittata (Page No: 88)
Tuesday	Almond butter muffins (Page No: 25)	Buffalo chicken strips (Page No: 44)	Keto Bacon Mini Frittata (Page No: 88)
Wednesday	Keto oatmeal (Page No: 23)	Carob Avocado Mousse (Page No: 75)	Paleo Lamb Meatballs (Page No: 74)
Thursday	Almond butter muffins (Page No: 25)	Chicken roulade (Page No: 50)	Shrimp & cauliflower curry (Page No: 73)
Friday	Keto green smoothie (Page No: 23)	Fried queso fresco (Page No: 61)	Egg & Bacon Sandwich (Page No: 78)
Saturday	Keto oatmeal (Page No: 23)	Carob Avocado Mousse (Page No: 75)	Paleo Lamb Meatballs (Page No: 74)

Breakfast recipes

Keto oatmeal

TIME TO PREPARE
Minutes

COOK TIME
Minutes

Serving
2 People

INGREDIENTS

- ¼ cup shredded coconut,
- Unsweetened ⅓ cup almonds,
- Flaked ¼ cup chia seeds
- ⅓ cup flaked coconut,
- Unsweetened 1 tsp.
- Unsweetened vanilla extract
- 1 cup hot water
- ½ cup of coconut milk
- 2 tbsp. Erythritol
- 6-8 drops stevia extract

INSTRUCTIONS

1. In a bowl, place the flaked and shredded coconut, almonds and chia seeds, setting aside a little bit of flaked coconut and almond.
2. Add the coconut milk, vanilla extract, stevia and combine. Add hot water and let sit for 10-15 minutes.
3. Sprinkle with flaked coconuts and almonds and top with berries

Nutrition Per Serving: Calories: 360, Fat: 30 g, Net Carbs: 5 g, Protein: 9.5 g

Keto green smoothie

TIME TO PREPARE
Minutes

COOK TIME
Minutes

Serving
1 People

INGREDIENTS

- 1½ cups almond milk
- 1 oz. Spinach
- ⅓ cup cucumber,
- Diced ⅓ cup celery,
- Diced ½ cup avocado,
- Diced 1 tbsp.
- Coconut oil Liquid stevia
- ¼ cup of protein powder

INSTRUCTIONS

1. Blend the almond milk and spinach in a blender.
2. Make room for the rest of the ingredients, and blend again until a smooth consistency is achieved.

Nutrition Per Serving: Calories: 370, Fat: 24g Net, Carbs: 5g, Protein: 27g

Breakfast recipes

Charismatic Crepes

TIME TO PREPARE
5 minutes

COOK TIME
15 minutes

Serving
4 People

INGREDIENTS

- 8 large eggs.
- Two cups thick whipping cream.
- ½ cup water (room temperature).
- 3 oz butter.

- 2 tbsp psyllium husk (powder).

INSTRUCTIONS

1. In a large bowl, whisk together eggs, cream, and water. Gradually mix in the psyllium husk until a smooth batter is formed. Allow resting for 20 minutes.
2. Use a little butter and ½ cup of batter mixture for one pancake.
3. When the top of the pancake is lightly browned and almost dry, flip and cook the other side.
4. Repeat until all batter has gone.

Nutrition Per Serving: Fat: 70g, Carbohydrates: 4g, Protein: 14g, Calories: 690

Breakfast recipes

Almond butter muffins

TIME TO PREPARE
10 minutes

COOK TIME
20 minutes

Serving
6 People

INGREDIENTS

- 2 cups almond flour
- 1 cup powdered erythritol
- Two teaspoons baking powder
- ¼ teaspoon salt
- ¾ cup almond butter, warmed
- ¾ cup unsweetened almond milk
- Four large eggs

INSTRUCTIONS

1. Preheat the oven to 350°f and line a muffin pan with paper liners.
2. Whisk the almond flour together with the erythritol, baking powder, and salt in a mixing bowl.
3. In a separate bowl, whisk together the almond milk, almond butter, and eggs.
4. Stir the wet ingredients into the dry until just combined.
5. Spoon the batter into the prepared pan and bake for 22 to 25 minutes until a knife inserted in the center comes out clean.
6. Cool the muffins in the pan for 5 minutes, then turn out onto a wire cooling rack.

Nutrition Per Serving: 135 calories, 11g fat, 6g protein, 4g carbs, 2g fiber, 2g net Carbs

Breakfast recipes

Blueberry Whirl Mousse

TIME TO PREPARE
10 minutes

COOK TIME
10 minutes

Serving
4 People

INGREDIENTS

- Two cups thick whipping cream.
- 3 oz blueberries (frozen & defrosted).
- 2 oz chopped walnuts.
- ½ lemon zest.
- ¼ tsp vanilla extract.

INSTRUCTIONS

1. In a bowl, whisk the cream, vanilla, and lemon zest until soft peaks are formed.
2. Stir in the walnuts until thoroughly combined.
3. Slightly crush the blueberries and gently swirl into the mousse.
4. Cover the bowl and place it in the refrigerator for 3-4 hours until mousse thickens.

Nutrition Per Serving: Fat: 27g, Carbohydrates: 3g, Protein: 3g, Calories: 257

Breakfast recipes

Shrimp Scampi Spinach Salad

TIME TO PREPARE
10 minutes

COOK TIME
20 minutes

Serving
4 People

INGREDIENTS

- Two tablespoons butter
- 1-pound uncooked shrimp (31-40 per pound), peeled and deveined
- Three garlic cloves, minced

- Two tablespoons chopped fresh parsley
- 6 ounces fresh baby spinach (about 8 cups)
- 1 cup cherry tomatoes, halved
- Lemon halves
- 1/8 teaspoon salt
- 1/8 teaspoon coarsely ground pepper
- 1/4 cup sliced almonds, toasted
- Shredded Parmesan cheese, optional

INSTRUCTIONS

1. In a large skillet, heat butter over medium heat; saute shrimp and garlic until shrimp turn pink, 3-4 minutes. Stir in parsley; remove from heat.
2. To serve, place spinach and tomatoes in a serving dish; top with shrimp mixture. Squeeze lemon juice over salad; sprinkle with salt and pepper. Sprinkle with almonds and, if desired, cheese.

Nutrition Per Serving: 201 calories, 10g fat, 153mg cholesterol, 291mg sodium, 21g protein

Breakfast recipes

Strawberry & Blueberry Yogurt Ice-cream

TIME TO PREPARE
5 minutes

COOK TIME
5 minutes

Serving
4 People

INGREDIENTS

- 8 oz strawberries (frozen & defrosted).
- 8 oz blueberries (frozen & defrosted).
- One cup of Greek yoghurt (full fat).
- ½ cup thick whipping cream.
- 1 tsp orange extract.

INSTRUCTIONS

1. Place all ingredients into a blender and mix until thoroughly combined.
2. Pour into a bowl and freeze for 40-60 minutes.

Nutrition Per Serving: Fat: 8g, Carbohydrates: 4g, Protein: 3g, Calories: 74

Breakfast recipes

Pumpkin Pie Custard

TIME TO PREPARE
5 minutes

COOK TIME
15 minutes

Serving
4 People

INGREDIENTS

- Four large egg yolks.
- 1 ½ cups thick whipping cream.
- 2 tbsp erythritol.
- 2 tsp pumpkin pie spice.
- ¼ tsp vanilla extract.

INSTRUCTIONS

1. Preheat the oven at 180 degrees.
2. In a saucepan, heat cream, erythritol, pumpkin pie spice, and vanilla extract; bring to the boil.
3. Place the egg yolks into a large bowl and gradually pour in the warm cream mixture, whisking continuously.
4. Pour into an ovenproof dish and place the ovenproof dish into a larger ovenproof dish. Add water to the giant bowl until it is halfway up the side of the first dish.
5. Bake for 25-30 minutes. Allow cooling before serving.

Nutrition Per Serving: Fat: 29g, Carbohydrates: 3g, Protein: 5g, Calories: 278

Breakfast recipes

Perfect Breakfast Pumpkin Bread

TIME TO PREPARE
5 minutes

COOK TIME
15 minutes

Serving
4 People

INGREDIENTS

- 4 large eggs.
- 1 ½ cups almond flour.
- ¾ cup pumpkin puree (canned).
- ⅔ cup erythritol.
- ½ cup softened butter.
- ½ cup coconut flour.
- 4 tsp baking powder.
- 1 tsp vanilla extract.
- 1 tsp cinnamon (ground).
- ½ tsp nutmeg (ground).
- ½ tsp salt.
- ¼ tsp ginger (ground).

INSTRUCTIONS

1. Preheat oven at 350 degrees.
2. Mix the butter and erythritol until light and creamy.
3. One at a time, whisk in eggs until all ingredients are well combined.
4. Mix in pumpkin puree and vanilla.
5. In another bowl, mix the almond flour, baking powder, coconut flour, cinnamon, nutmeg, ginger, and salt.
6. Add the flour mixture to the egg mixture; stir until well combined.
7. Line a 9 x 5-inch loaf pan with greaseproof paper and pour in the butter mixture.
8. Bake for 45 -50 minutes or until a skewer inserted in the middle comes out clean.

Nutrition Per Serving: Fat: 14g, Carbohydrates: 6g, Protein: 5g, Calories: 166g

Breakfast recipes

PEANUT BUTTER MUFFINS

TIME TO PREPARE
Minutes

COOK TIME
Minutes

Serving
2 People

INGREDIENTS

- ½ cup erythritol
- 1 cup almond flour
- 1 tbsp. Baking powder
- ⅓ cup almond milk
- ⅓ cup peanut butter
- 2 eggs
- ½ cup sugar-free chocolate chips Salt

INSTRUCTIONS

1. Mix the erythritol, almond flour, and baking powder in a bowl and whisk.
2. Add the peanut butter and almond milk, and stir.
3. Add in the first egg and combine well. Add the second and combine well.
4. Fold in the chocolate chips.
5. Place the muffins in a muffin tin (of 6 cups) and bake them on 350°F for 15 minutes and cool.

Nutrition Per Serving: Calories: 527, Fat: 40g, Net Carbs: 4.3g, Protein: 14g

Breakfast recipes

Cheesy Frittata Muffins

TIME TO PREPARE
10 minutes

COOK TIME
15 minutes

Serving
4 People

INGREDIENTS

- 4 Large Eggs
- 1/2 Cup Half n' Half
- 4 Oz. Bacon (pre-cooked and chopped)
- 1/2 Cup Cheddar Cheese
- 1 Tbsp. Butter
- 2 tsp. Dried Parsley
- 1/2 tsp. Pepper
- 1/4 tsp. Salt

INSTRUCTIONS

1. Preheat oven to 375 degrees
2. Mix eggs and half n' half in a bowl until almost scrambled, leaving streaks of egg white
3. Fold in the bacon, cheese, and spices. Add any other additional ingredients now
4. Grease a muffin tin with butter. This recipe makes about 8 frittata muffins.
5. Pour the mixture, filling each cup about 3/4 way.
6. Stick them in the oven for 15-18 minutes, or until puffy and golden on the edges.
7. Remove from the oven and let cool for 1 minute. These freeze well and can be heated individually.

Nutrition Per Serving: 205 Calories, 16.1g Fats, 1.3g Net Carbs, and 13.6g Protein.

Breakfast recipes

Cheesy Scrambled Eggs

TIME TO PREPARE
5 minutes

COOK TIME
10 minutes

Serving
2 People

INGREDIENTS

- 2 Large Eggs
- 2 Tbsp. Butter 1 Oz.
- Cheddar Cheese

INSTRUCTIONS

1. Heat a pan on the stove, adding the butter.
2. Once the butter has melted, add 2 eggs that have been scrambled.
3. Let the eggs cook slowly, only touching them once or twice throughout the whole process.
4. Add cheese and mix everything together.

Nutrition Per Serving: 453 Calories, 43g Fats, 1.2g Net Carbs, and 19g Protein.

Breakfast recipes
Almond Lemon Cake Sandwiches

TIME TO PREPARE
5 minutes

COOK TIME
20 minutes

Serving
6 People

INGREDIENTS

Almond Lemon Cakes

- 1/4 Cup Honeyville Almond Flour
- 1/4 Cup Coconut Flour
- 1/4 Cup Butter
- 3 Large Eggs
- 1/4 Cup Erythritol
- 1 Tbsp. Lemon Juice
- 1 Tbsp. Coconut Milk

- 1 tsp. Cinnamon
- 1/2 tsp. Almond Extract
- 1/2 tsp. Vanilla Extract
- 1/2 tsp. Baking Soda
- 1/2 tsp. Apple Cider Vinegar
- 1/4 tsp. Liquid Stevia 1
- /4 tsp. Salt

Sandwich Icing

- 1/4 Cup Powdered Erythritol
- 4 Oz. Cream Cheese
- 4 Tbsp. Butter

- 2 Tbsp. Heavy Cream
- 1 tsp. Red Food Coloring

INSTRUCTIONS

1. Preheat your oven to 325F.
2. Sift and mix coconut flour, almond flour, cinnamon salt, and baking soda.
3. Combine eggs, erythritol, vanilla extract, almond extract, lemon juice, melted butter, coconut milk, vinegar, stevia, and food coloring.
4. Mix the wet ingredients into the dry ingredients, using a hand mixer until it is fluffy.
5. Divide your batter between your a muffin top pan and bake for 1718 minutes.
6. Remove from the oven and let cool on a cooling rack for 10 minutes.
7. Slice cakes in half and fry them in butter until crisped.
8. Let cool on cooling rack again.
9. Mix together butter, cream cheese, heavy cream, and powdered erythritol until fluffy. Add food coloring until color is attained.

10. Divide icing in between middle of the cakes and make a sandwich. Garnish with lemon zest and pistachios.

Nutrition Per Serving: 180 Calories, 17.5g Fats, 1.8g Net Carbs, and 2.8g Protein.

Breakfast recipes

Breakfast tacos

TIME TO PREPARE
Minutes

COOK TIME
Minutes

Serving
3 People

INGREDIENTS

- 1 cup mozzarella cheese
- 6 eggs
- 2 tbsp butter
- 3 strips of bacon
- 1 oz. Cheddar cheese,
- ½ an avocado
- Salt and pepper

INSTRUCTIONS

1. Cook the bacon on a baking sheet covered with aluminium foil at 375°F, until crispy (12-15 minutes).
2. Meanwhile, use a third of the mozzarella to cover the bottom of a nonstick pan. Heat for 2-3 minutes on medium heat, or until the edges begin to brown.
3. With a pair of tongs, remove the mozzarella from the pan (it will now be a taco shell). Repeat with the remaining cheese.
4. Scramble the eggs in the butter. Stir frequently, and add pepper and salt to taste.
5. Fill the shells with the eggs, avocado and bacon. Sprinkle cheddar cheese on the top. Add hot sauce or cilantro (optional).

Nutrition Per Serving: Calories: 440, Fat: 36g, Net Carbs: 4g, Protein: 26g

Breakfast recipes

Classic western omelet

TIME TO PREPARE
5 minutes

COOK TIME
10 minutes

Serving
1 People

INGREDIENTS

- Two teaspoons coconut oil
- Three large eggs whisked
- One tablespoon heavy cream
- Salt and pepper
- ¼ cup diced green pepper
- ¼ cup diced yellow onion
- ¼ cup diced ham

INSTRUCTIONS

1. Whisk together the eggs, heavy cream, salt, and pepper in a small bowl.
2. Heat 1 teaspoon coconut oil in a small skillet over medium heat.
3. Add the peppers, onions, and ham, then sauté for 3 to 4 minutes.
4. Spoon the mixture into a bowl and reheat the skillet with the rest of the oil.
5. Pour in the whisked eggs and cook until the bottom of the egg starts to set.
6. Tilt the pan to spread the egg and cook until almost set.
7. Spoon the veggie and ham mixture over half the omelet and fold it over.
8. Let the omelet cook until the eggs set, then serve hot.

Nutrition Per Serving: 415 calories, 32.5g fat, 25g protein, 6.5g carbs, 1.5g fiber, 5g net carbs

Breakfast recipes

Cheddar scrambled eggs

TIME TO PREPARE
5 minutes

COOK TIME
15 minutes

Serving
1 People

INGREDIENTS

- 4 cup fresh spinach
- 4 eggs ½ cup cheddar cheese
- 1 tbsp. Heavy cream
- 1 tbsp. Olive oil
- Salt and pepper

INSTRUCTIONS

1. In a bowl, mix together the eggs, heavy cream, salt and pepper.
2. Heat a large pan and add the olive oil and spinach when the oil is heated.
3. Stir the spinach and add the salt and pepper.
4. Once the spinach is fairly wilted, add the egg mixture and turn to medium heat.
5. When the eggs are set, add the cheese and stir slowly until it melts.

Nutrition Per Serving: Calories: 700, Fat: 58g, Net Carbs: 5g, Protein: 43g

Breakfast recipes

Inside Out Bacon Burger

TIME TO PREPARE
10 minutes

COOK TIME
15 minutes

Serving
2 People

INGREDIENTS

- 200g Ground Beef
- 2 Slices Bacon
- 2 Tbsp. Cheddar Cheese

- 1 1/2 tsp. Chopped Chives
- 1/2 tsp. Minced Garlic
- 1/2 tsp. Black Pepper

- 3/4 tsp. Soy Sauce
- 1/2 tsp. Salt
- 1/4 tsp. Onion Powder
- 1/4 tsp. Worcestershire

INSTRUCTIONS

1. In a cast iron skillet, cook all your chopped bacon until crisp. Once cooked, remove and place on paper towel. Drain grease separately and save.
2. In a large mixing bowl, combine ground beef, 2/3 chopped bacon, and the rest of the spices.
3. Mix meat and spices together well, then form into 3 patties.
4. Put 2 Tbsp. Bacon fat into cast iron and place patties inside once fat is hot.
5. Cook about 4-5 minutes on each side, depending on the done-ness you want.
6. Remove from pan, let rest for 3-5 minutes, and serve with cheese, extra bacon, and onion if you'd like.

Nutrition Per Serving: 649 Calories, 51.8g Fats, 1.8g Net Carbs, and 43.5g Protein.

Breakfast recipes

Quick keto scramble

TIME TO PREPARE
Minutes

COOK TIME
Minutes

Serving
1 People

INGREDIENTS

- 3 eggs,
- Whisked 4 baby Bella mushrooms
- ¼ cup red bell peppers
- ½ cup spinach
- 2 slices deli ham
- 1 tbsp. Coconut oil
- Salt and pepper

INSTRUCTIONS

1. Mince the vegetables and the ham.
2. Brown them in a frying pan with melted butter.
3. Add the eggs and seasonings, and scramble the eggs until cooked through.

Nutrition Per Serving: Calories: 350, Fat: 30g, Net Carbs: 5g, Protein: 20g

Breakfast recipes

Bacon & Mozzarella Meatballs

TIME TO PREPARE
10 minutes

COOK TIME
30 minutes

Serving
4 People

INGREDINTS

1 1/2 lb. Ground Beef
4 Slices Bacon
1 Cup Mozzarella Cheese
3/4 Cup Pesto Sauce
1/3 Cup Crushed Pork Rinds

2 Large Eggs
1 tsp. Pepper
2 tsp. Minced Garlic
1/2 tsp. Onion Powder
1/2 tsp. Kosher Salt

INSTRUCTIONS

1. Preheat oven to 350F.
2. Slice your bacon into small pieces (almost into small cubes).
3. Add your ground beef, ground pork rinds, spices, cheese, and eggs to the bacon.
4. Mix everything together well until you can form meatballs.
5. Roll your meatballs out into circles and place them in a foiled baking tray.
6. Bake in the oven for 40-45 minutes, or until bacon is cooked.
7. Spoon out 1/2 Tbsp. Pesto sauce per meatball and serve.

Nutrition Per Serving: 128 Calories, 9.4g Fats, 0.7g Net Carbs, and 10.1g Protein.

Breakfast recipes

BROWNIE MUFFINS

TIME TO PREPARE
10 minutes

COOK TIME
10 minutes

Serving
6 People

INGREDIENTS

- 1 cup golden flaxseed meal
- 1 tbsp. Cinnamon

- ¼ cup cocoa powder
- ½ tsp. Salt
- ½ tsp. Baking powder
- 1 egg
- 2 tbsp. Coconut oil
- ¼ cup sugar-free caramel syrup
- ½ cup pumpkin purée
- 1 tbsp. Vanilla extract
- 1 tbsp. Apple cider vinegar
- ¼ cup slivered almonds

INSTRUCTIONS

1. Preheat oven to 350°F.
2. Place all the ingredients except the almonds into a large mixing bowl, and combine well.
3. In a lined muffin pan, fill each space, dividing the batter into 6 parts.
4. Sprinkle the almonds on top.
5. Bake for around 15 minutes.

Nutrition Per Serving: Calories: 185, Fat: 13.5g, Net Carbs: 3.5g, Protein: 7.4g

Breakfast recipes

Bacon Infused Sugar Snap Peas

TIME TO PREPARE
10 minutes

COOK TIME
15 minutes

Serving
3 People

INGREDIENTS

- 3 cups sugar snap peas (~200g)
- 1/2 lemon juice
- 3 tbsp. Bacon fat
- 2 tsp. Garlic
- 1/2 tsp. Red pepper flakes

INSTRUCTIONS

1. Add 3 tbsp. Bacon fat to a pan and bring to its smoking point.

2. Add your garlic and reduce heat on the pan, letting the garlic cook for 1-2 minutes.
3. Add sugar snap peas and lemon juice, let cook for 1-2 minutes.
4. Remove and serve. Garnish with red pepper flakes and lemon zest.

Nutrition Per Serving: 147 calories, 13.3g fats, 4.3g net carbs, and 1.3g protein.

Breakfast recipes

Breakfast burgers

TIME TO PREPARE
Minutes

COOK TIME
Minutes

Serving
2 People

INGREDIENTS

- 4 oz. Sausage
- 2 oz. Pepper jack cheese
- 4 slices bacon
- 2 eggs
- 1 tbsp. Butter
- 1 tbsp. Peanut butter powder Salt and pepper

INSTRUCTIONS

1. Bake the bacon on a cooking sheet at 400°F for 20-25 minutes.
2. Combine the butter and peanut butter powder in a small bowl.
3. Form 2 patties from the sausage, and cook them until well done.
4. Add cheese, and cover with a lid so that it melts. Remove from the pan.
5. Cook the egg and set atop the burger along with the peanut butter mix and bacon slices.

Nutrition Per Serving: Calories: 652, Fat: 55g, Net Carbs: 3g, Protein: 30g

Mushroom Soup with Fried egg

TIME TO PREPARE
5 minutes

COOK TIME
15 minutes

Serving
4 People

INGREDIENTS

- One teaspoon olive oil
- Four white mushrooms, sliced thin
- 100 grams cauliflower, riced
- 1 cup vegetable broth
- Three tablespoons heavy cream
- Two tablespoons shredded cheese
- One teaspoon butter
- Four large egg

INSTRUCTIONS

1. Heat the oil in a small saucepan over medium heat.
2. Add the mushrooms and cook until they are tender about 6 minutes.
3. Stir in the riced cauliflower, vegetable broth, and heavy cream.
4. Season with salt and pepper, then stir in the cheese.
5. Simmer the soup until it thickens to the desired level, then remove from heat.
6. Fry the egg in the butter until cooked to the desired level, then serve over the soup.

Nutrition Per Serving: Calories: 385, Fat: 31 g, Protein: 20 g, Fiber: 3 g, Net Carbs: 7 g

Breakfast recipes

Sausage and egg scramble

TIME TO PREPARE
Minutes

COOK TIME
Minutes

Serving
1 People

INGREDIENTS

- 1 cup red bell pepper,
- 1 cup onion
- 4 eggs
- 3 spicy chicken sausages
- ¼ cup mozzarella cheese,
- 1 tsp. Cayenne
- Pepper powder Salt

INSTRUCTIONS

1. Place the chopped red bell peppers and onion into a skillet. Sauté until the onion starts to turn transparent, and then add the chicken sausage (chopped into small pieces).
2. Sauté just long enough to heat the sausage.
3. Add the eggs and mozzarella cheese, and mix with a spatula.
4. Scramble for a further 3-4 minutes, or until the mixture has finished cooking.
5. Add the cayenne pepper and salt to taste.

Nutrition Per Serving: Calories: 750, Fat: 40g, Net Carbs: 17g, Protein: 75g

Avocado Egg & salami sandwiches

TIME TO PREPARE

5 minutes

COOK TIME

10 minutes

Serving

4 People

INGREDIENTS

- 4 Easy Cloud Buns
- One teaspoon butter
- Four large eggs
- One medium tomato, sliced into four slices
- 1-ounce fresh mozzarella, sliced thin
- One small avocado, sliced thin
- 2 ounces sliced salami
- Salt and pepper

INSTRUCTIONS

1. Toast the cloud buns on a baking sheet in the oven until golden brown.
2. Heat the butter in a large skillet over medium heat.
3. Crack the eggs into the skillet and season with salt and pepper.
4. Cook the eggs until done to the desired level, then place one on each cloud bun.
5. Top the buns with sliced tomato, mozzarella, avocado, and salami.

Nutrition Per Serving: Calories: 490 Fat: 40.5 g Protein: 22.5 g Fiber: 7.5 g Net Carbs: 5 g

Breakfast recipes

Crepes with blueberries

TIME TO PREPARE

Minutes

COOK TIME

Minutes

Serving

6 People

INGREDIENTS

- 2 oz. Cream cheese
- 2 eggs
- 10 drops liquid stevia
- ¼ tsp. Cinnamon
- ¼ tsp. Baking soda
- ⅛ tsp. Salt For the Filling
- 4 oz. Cream cheese
- ½ tsp. Vanilla extract
- 2 tsp. Powdered erythritol
- ½ cup blueberries

INSTRUCTIONS

1. In a bowl, mix the cream cheese and eggs with an electric hand mixer until smooth.
2. Add the stevia, cinnamon, baking soda and salt, and mix.
3. Add butter or coconut oil in a nonstick pan, and heat over medium. Pour in some batter – to make a very thin layer - and cook for 3 minutes. Flip the crepe, cook for a further minute, and remove.
4. Make the filling: combine the cream cheese, vanilla extract and powdered erythritol, and stir with the electric mixer until creamy.
5. Add the filling, cinnamon and blueberries to your crepes and either fold or roll them up.

Nutrition Per Serving: Calories: 400, Fat: 35g, Net Carbs: 6g, Protein: 15g

Breakfast recipes

Crispy chai waffles

TIME TO PREPARE
10 minutes

COOK TIME
20 minutes

Serving
4 People

INGREDIENTS

- Four large eggs, separated into whites and yolks
- Three tablespoons coconut flour
- Three tablespoons powdered erythritol
- One ¼ teaspoon baking powder
- One teaspoon vanilla extract
- ½ teaspoon ground cinnamon
- ¼ teaspoon ground ginger
- Pinch ground cloves
- Pinch ground cardamom
- Three tablespoons coconut oil, melted
- Three tablespoons unsweetened almond milk

INSTRUCTIONS

1. Separate the eggs into two different mixing bowls.
2. Whip the egg whites until stiff peaks form then set aside.
3. Whisk the egg yolks with the coconut flour, erythritol, baking powder, vanilla, cinnamon, cardamom, and cloves in the other bowl.
4. Add the melted coconut oil to the second bowl while whisking, then whisk in the almond milk.
5. Gently fold in the egg whites until just combined.
6. Preheat the waffle iron and grease with cooking spray.
7. Spoon about ½ cup of batter into the iron.
8. Cook the waffle according to the manufacturer's instructions.
9. Remove the waffle to a plate and repeat with the remaining batter.

Nutrition Per Serving: 215 calories, 17g fat, 8g protein, 8g carbs, 4g fiber, 4g net carbs

Lunch recipes

Tantalizingly Tasty Tomato

TIME TO PREPARE
5 minutes

COOK TIME
10 minutes

Serving
6 People

INGREDIENTS

- 8 oz cream cheese (softened).
- Two cans tomatoes (chopped).
- Four cups of chicken broth.
- One cup parmesan (grated).
- ½ cup red onions (finely chopped).
- 2 tbsp coconut oil.
- Two garlic cloves (crushed).
- 1 tbsp basil (dried).
- 1 tsp oregano (dried).
- 1 tsp salt.
- ½ tsp black pepper.

INSTRUCTIONS

1. In a large pan, place the coconut oil, onions, garlic, basil, and oregano; cook over medium heat until onions are softened.

2. Add in cream cheese, stirring continuously.
3. Gradually add the broth, tomatoes, parmesan, salt, and Pepper.
4. Cover and simmer for 8-10 minutes.
5. Pour soup into a blender and blend until pureed.

Nutrition Per Serving: Fat: 12g, Carbohydrates: 3g, Protein: 7g, Calories: 149

Lunch recipes

Buffalo chicken strips

TIME TO PREPARE
10 minutes

COOK TIME
20 minutes

Serving
6 People

INGREDIENTS

- 5 chicken breasts pounded to
- 1/2" thickness
- 3/4 cup almond flour
- 1/2 cup hot sauce
- 1/4 cup olive oil
- 3 tbsp. Butter
- 3 tbsp. Blue cheese crumbles

- 2 large eggs
- 1 tbsp. Paprika
- 1 tbsp. Chili powder
- 2 tsp. Salt
- 2 tsp. Pepper
- 1 tsp. Garlic powder
- 1 tsp. Onion powder

INSTRUCTIONS

1. Preheat oven to 400f.
2. In a ramekin, combine paprika, chili powder, salt, pepper, garlic powder, and onion powder.
3. Pound out chicken breasts to 1/2" thickness, then cut the chicken breasts in half.
4. Sprinkle 1/3 of the spice mix over the chicken breast, then flip them over and do the same with 1/3 of the spice mix.
5. In a bowl, combine almond flour and 1/3 of the spice mix.
6. In another container, crack 2 eggs and whisk them.
7. Dip each piece of seasoned chicken into the spice mix and then into the almond flour. Make sure each side is coated well.
8. Lay each piece on a cooling rack on top of a foiled baking sheet.
9. Bake the chicken for 15 minutes.
10. Take the chicken out of the oven and turn your oven to broil. Drizzle 2 tbsp. Olive oil over the chicken.

11. Broil for 5 minutes, flip the breasts, drizzle with remaining olive oil, and broil again for 5 minutes.
12. In a sauce pan, combined 1/2 cup of hot sauce with 3 tbsp. Butter.
13. Serve chicken with slathering of hot sauce and blue cheese crumbles.

Nutrition Per Serving: 683 calories, 54g fats, 4.8g net carbs, and 41g protein.

Lunch recipes

Bacon cheddar explosion

TIME TO PREPARE
10 minutes

COOK TIME
45 minutes

Serving
4 People

INGREDIENTS

- 30 slices of bacon
- 2 1/2 cups cheddar cheese
- 4-5 cups raw spinach
- 1-2 tbsp. Tones southwest chipotle seasoning
- 2 tsp. Mrs. Dash table seasoning

INSTRUCTIONS

1. Preheat your oven to 375f convection bake. (400f regular bake)
2. Weave the bacon. 15 pieces that are vertical, 12 pieces horizontal, And the extra 3 cut in half to fill in rest, horizontally.
3. Season your bacon with your favorite seasoning mix.
4. Add your cheese to the bacon, leaving about 1 1/2 inch gaps between the edges.
5. Add your spinach and press down on it to compress it some. This will help when you roll it up.
6. Roll your weave slowly, making sure it stays tight and not too much falls through. You may have some cheese fall out, but don't worry about it. Add your seasoning to the outside here, if you'd like.
7. Foil a baking sheet and add plenty of salt to it. This will help catch excess grease from the bacon and not let your oven smoke.
8. Put your bacon on top of a cooling rack and put that on top of your baking sheet.
9. Bake for 60-70 minutes, without opening the oven door. Your bacon should be very crisp on the top when finished.
10. Let cool for 10-15 minutes before trying to take it off the cooling rack. Slice into pieces, and serve!

Nutrition Per Serving: 720 calories, 63.7g fats, 4.9g net carbs, and 54.7g protein.

Lunch recipes

Eggs with Asparagus

TIME TO PREPARE
5 minutes

COOK TIME
15 minutes

Serving
4 People

INGREDIENTS

- 2 pounds asparagus
- 1-pint cherry tomatoes
- Four eggs
- Two tablespoons olive oil
- Two teaspoons chopped fresh thyme
- Salt and Pepper to taste

INSTRUCTIONS

1. Preheat the oven to 400°F. Grease a baking sheet with non-stick cooking spray.
2. Arrange the asparagus and cherry tomatoes in an even layer on the baking sheet. Drizzle the olive oil over the vegetables; season with the thyme and salt and Pepper to taste.
3. Roast in the oven until the asparagus is nearly tender and the tomatoes are wrinkled, 10 to 12 minutes.
4. Crack the eggs on top of the asparagus; season each with salt and Pepper.
5. Return to the oven and bake until the egg whites are set but the yolks are still jiggly, 7 to 8 minutes more.
6. To serve, divide the asparagus, tomatoes, and eggs among four plates.

Nutrition Per Serving: 158 calories,11g fat,13g carbs,11g protein,7g sugars

Lunch recipes

Cheddar chorizo meatballs

TIME TO PREPARE
10 minutes

COOK TIME
35 minutes

Serving
2 People

INGREDIENTS

- 1 1/2 lb. Ground beef
- 1 1/2 chorizo sausages
- 1 cup cheddar cheese
- 1 cup tomato sauce
- 1/3 cup crushed pork rinds
- 2 large eggs 1 tsp. Cumin
- 1 tsp. Chili powder
- 1 tsp. Kosher salt

INSTRUCTIONS

1. Preheat oven to 350f.
2. Break up sausage into small pieces so that it will mix well with the ground beef.
3. Add your ground beef, ground pork rinds, spices, cheese, and eggs to the sausage.
4. Mix everything together well until you can form meatballs.
5. Roll your meatballs out into circles and place them in a foiled baking tray.
6. Bake in the oven for 30-35 minutes, or until meatballs are cooked through.
7. Spoon tomato sauce over meatballs and serve.

Nutrition Per Serving: 115 calories, 7.8g fats, 0.8g net carbs, and 9.9g protein.

Lunch recipes

Cheesy scrambled eggs

TIME TO PREPARE
5 minutes

COOK TIME
15 minutes

Serving
2 People

INGREDIENTS

- 2 large eggs
- 2 tbsp. Butter
- 1 oz. Cheddar cheese

INSTRUCTIONS

1. Heat a pan on the stove, adding the butter.
2. Once the butter has melted, add 2 eggs that have been scrambled.
3. Let the eggs cook slowly, only touching them once or twice throughout the whole process.
4. Add cheese and mix everything together.

Nutrition Per Serving: 453 calories, 43g fats, 1.2g net carbs, and 19g protein.

Lunch recipes

Cheesy spinach

TIME TO PREPARE
5 minutes

COOK TIME
15 minutes

Serving
2 People

INGREDIENTS

- 7 cups spinach
- 1 1/2 cup cheddar cheese
- 3 tbsp. Butter
- 1/2 tsp. Mrs. Dash
- 1/2 tsp. Salt
- 1/2 tsp. Pepper

INSTRUCTIONS

1. Heat a pan on the stove, adding the butter.
2. Once the butter has melted, add spinach and spices. Let the spinach begin to wilt.
3. Once the spinach is almost completely wilted, add shredded cheese to the top and let it all melt together.
4. Once melted, serve.

Nutrition Per Serving: 446 calories, 47g fats, 4.8g net carbs, and 24g protein.

Lunch recipes

Greek Wedge

TIME TO PREPARE
5 minutes

COOK TIME
10 minutes

Serving
4 People

INGREDIENTS

- ½ cup extra-virgin olive oil
- One tablespoon Dijon mustard
- One garlic clove, minced
- One teaspoon dried oregano
- One teaspoon salt
- ¾ teaspoon freshly ground Black Pepper
- ⅓ cup red wine vinegar

INSTRUCTIONS

1. In a medium bowl, whisk the olive oil with the mustard, garlic, oregano, salt, and Pepper. Gradually whisk in the red wine vinegar and mix well to combine.
2. Garnish with two tablespoons feta, ¼ cup olives, and a peperoncino pepper. Serve immediately.

Nutrition Per Serving: 248 calories,27g fat,1g carbs,0g protein,0g sugars

Lunch recipes

Cheesy Spinach

TIME TO PREPARE
5 minutes

COOK TIME
10 minutes

Serving
2 People

INGREDIENTS

- 7 Cups Spinach
- 1 1/2 Cup Cheddar Cheese
- 3 Tbsp. Butter
- 1/2 tsp. Mrs. Dash
- 1/2 tsp. Salt
- 1/2 tsp. Pepper

INSTRUCTIONS

1. Heat a pan on the stove, adding the butter.
2. Once the butter has melted, add spinach and spices. Let the spinach begin to wilt.
3. Once the spinach is almost completely wilted,
4. Add shredded cheese to the top and let it all melt together.
5. Once melted, serve

Nutrition Per Serving:446 Calories, 47g Fats, 4.8g Net Carbs, and 24g Protein.

Lunch recipes

Chicken roulade

TIME TO PREPARE
10 minutes

COOK TIME
15 minutes

Serving
2 People

INGREDIENTS

- 2 chicken breasts
- 1 tbsp. Pesto
- 2 tsp. Olive oil zest
- 1 lemon
- 1 tsp. Garlic 38g halloumi cheese

INSTRUCTIONS

1. Pat your chicken breast dries of any extra moisture. Pound the chicken breast to 1/8".
2. Mix together pesto and 1 1/4 tsp. Olive oil. Spread the mixture out
3. On all the chicken breast.
4. Add salt, pepper, and lemon zest to each chicken.
5. Add sliced halloumi cheese to chicken breast.
6. Roll the chicken breast up and tie them using butchers string or toothpicks.
7. Preheat oven to 450f.
8. Heat 1 tsp. Olive oil in a cast iron to high heat.
9. Sear each side of the chicken making sure it gets nice and brown.
10. Bake for 6-7 minutes until juice runs clear.

Nutrition Per Serving: 478 calories, 31g fats, 2.5g net carbs, and 53.3g protein.

Lunch recipes

Cloud Nine BLT

TIME TO PREPARE
5 minutes

COOK TIME
10 minutes

Serving
2 People

INGREDIENTS

Bread:

- 4 ½ oz cream cheese (softened).
- Three large eggs.
- ½ tbsp psyllium husk powder.
- ½ tsp baking powder.
- Pinch of salt.

Fillings:

- 5 oz cooked bacon (grilled).
- 2 oz lettuce.
- One tomato (sliced).
- ½ cup mayonnaise.

INSTRUCTIONS

1. Preheat oven at 300 degrees.
2. Crack the eggs, putting egg whites in one bowl and yolks in another.
3. Add the salt to the egg whites and whisk until stiff peaks are formed.
4. Add the cream cheese to the egg yolks and stir well. Add psyllium husk and baking powder; mix until well combined.
5. Fold the egg white mixture into the egg yolk mixture.
6. Line a baking tray with greaseproof paper.
7. Make eight dough balls and place on the tray; flatten each one.
8. Bake for 25 minutes or until golden brown.
9. Place a slice of bread (topside down) on a serving plate and spread with mayonnaise.
10. Layer the bacon, lettuce, and tomato on to the bread; add a spoon of mayonnaise and top with the final slice of bread.

Nutrition Per Serving: Fat: 48g, Carbohydrates: 4g, Protein: 12g, Calories: 499g

Lunch recipes

Buffalo chicken strip slider

TIME TO PREPARE
10 minutes

COOK TIME
20 minutes

Serving
4 People

INGREDIENTS

Almond flour buns

- 1/3 cup almond flour
- 1/4 cup flax seed
- 3 tbsp. Parmesan cheese
- 2 large eggs 4 tbsp. Butter
- 1 tsp. Baking soda
- 1 tsp. Southwest seasoning
- 1 tsp. Paprika 1/2 tsp. Apple cider vinegar

Chicken filling

- 2 leftover buffalo chicken strips

INSTRUCTIONS

1. Preheat oven to 350f.
2. Mix together all dry ingredients in a large mixing bowl.
3. Melt butter in the microwave, then add eggs, vinegar, stevia and butter to mixture.
4. Mix everything well and spread the mixture out between 8 muffin top slots in a pan.
5. Bake for 15-17 minutes. Once baked, let cool for 5 minutes, then cut buns in half.
6. Assemble slider together with bun, and buffalo chicken strips.

Nutrition Per Serving: 625 calories, 51g fats, 4.3g net carbs, and 34.8g protein.

Lunch recipes

Bacon, cheddar & chive mug biscuit

TIME TO PREPARE
5 minutes

COOK TIME
10 minutes

Serving
2 People

INGREDIENTS

Base

- 2 egg
- 2 tbsp. Butter
- 2 tbsp. Almond flour
- 1 tsp. Baking powder

Flavor
- 2 slices bacon
- 1 tbsp. Almond flour
- 1 tbsp. Packed shredded cheddar
- 1 tbsp. Packed shredded white cheddar
- 1 tbsp. Chopped chive pinch salt
- 1/4 tsp. Mrs. Dash

INSTRUCTIONS

1. Mix all room temperature ingredients together in a mug.
2. Microwave on high for 70 seconds.
3. Turn cup upside down and lightly bang it against a plate.
4. Optional: let cool for 3-4 minutes.

Nutrition Per Serving: 573 calories, 55g fats, 5g net carbs, and 24g protein.

Lunch recipes

Pure Perfection Pepperoni Pizza

TIME TO PREPARE
5 minutes

COOK TIME
20 minutes

Serving
2 People

INGREDIENTS

- 4 large eggs.
- 6 oz mozzarella (grated)

Topping:

- 3 tbsp tomato puree.
- 5 oz mozzarella (grated).
- 1 ½ oz pepperoni (sliced).
- ½ tsp dried mixed herbs.

INSTRUCTIONS

1. Preheat oven at 400 degrees.
2. Mix the eggs with 6oz grated mozzarella, until well combined.
3. Line a baking tray with greaseproof paper. I was using a spatula, spread mixture into one large rectangular pizza.
4. Bake for 15-20 minutes until lightly browned. Remove from the oven.
5. Adjust oven temperature to 450 degrees.
6. Spread tomato puree on to the pizza and sprinkle on the herbs. Load with the remaining cheese and place pepperoni on top.
7. Bake for an additional 10 minutes or until golden brown and cheese has melted.

Nutrition Per Serving: Fat: 90g, Carbohydrates: 5g, Protein: 52g, Calories: 1043g

Lunch recipes

Cinnamon & orange beef stew

TIME TO PREPARE
15 minutes

COOK TIME
45 minutes

Serving
2 People

INGREDIENTS

- 1/4-pound beef
- 3/4 cup beef broth
- 1 tbsp. Coconut oil
- 1/4 medium onion
- Zest of 1/4 orange
- Juice of 1/4 orange
- 3/4 tsp. Fresh thyme
- 3/4 tsp. Minced garlic
- 1/2 tsp. Ground cinnamon
- 1/2 tsp. Soy sauce
- 1/2 tsp. Fish sauce
- 1/4 tsp. Rosemary
- 1/4 tsp. Sage 1 bay leaf

INSTRUCTIONS

1. Dice your vegetables, cut your meat into approximate 1" cubes. And zest a whole orange.
2. Heat coconut oil in a cast iron skillet, waiting for it to get to the smoke point.
3. Add your seasoned (salt and pepper) meat to the skillet in batches. Don't overfill the skillet. Brown the beef and remove from the cast iron, then add more beef to brown.
4. Once your beef is finished browning, remove the last batch and add your vegetables. Let these cook for 1-2 minutes.
5. Add your orange juice to de-glaze the pan and then add all other ingredients except for the rosemary, sage, and thyme.
6. Let this cook for a moment, and then transfer all ingredients to your crock pot.
7. Let this cook for 3 hours on high.
8. Open your crock pot and add the rest of your spices. Let this cook down for 1-2 hours on high.

Nutrition Per Serving: 649 calories, 44.5g fats, 1.9g net carbs, and 53.5g protein.

Lunch recipes

Intense Cauliflower Cheese Bake

TIME TO PREPARE
5 minutes

COOK TIME
15 minutes

Serving
2 People

INGREDIENTS

- 1 large cauliflower head.
- 8 oz thick cream.
- 4 oz cheddar (grated).
- 4 oz mozzarella (grated).
- 3 oz cream cheese (softened).
- 1 ½ tsp paprika.
- 1 tsp salt.
- ½ tsp black pepper.

INSTRUCTIONS

1. Preheat oven at 375 degrees.
2. Cut cauliflower into 1-inch pieces and steam for 5 minutes until just becoming tender.
3. In a medium-sized pan, combine thick cream, cheddar, mozzarella, cream cheese, salt, pepper, and paprika. Over medium heat, I was stirring continuously, until a smooth sauce is formed.
4. Add the cauliflower to a baking dish and pour over the cheese sauce; stir to ensure all cauliflower is covered.
5. Bake for 30 minutes or until the top is bubbling and golden.

Nutrition Per Serving: Fat: 33g, Carbohydrates: 11g, Protein: 15g, Calories: 393g

Lunch recipes

Coffee & red wine beef stew

TIME TO PREPARE
10 minutes

COOK TIME
35 minutes

Serving
4 People

INGREDIENTS

- 2.5 pounds stew meat
- 3 cups coffee
- 1 cup beef stock
- 1 1/2 cup mushrooms
- 2/3 cup red wine (merlot)
- 1 medium onion
- 3 tbsp. Coconut oil
- 2 tbsp. Capers
- 2 tsp. Garlic

INSTRUCTIONS

1. Cube all stew meat, then thinly slice onions and mushrooms.
2. Bring 3 tbsp. Coconut oil to its smoking point in a pan on the stove.
3. Season beef with salt and pepper, then brown all of it in small batches, making sure that the pan isn't overcrowded.
4. Once all meat is browned, cook onions, mushrooms, and garlic in the remaining fat in the pan. Do this until onions are translucent.
5. Add coffee, beef stock, red wine, and capers to the vegetables and stir this mixture.
6. Add beef into the mixture, bring to a boil then reduce heat to low.
7. Cover and cook for 3 hours.

Nutrition Per Serving: 755 calories, 48.3g fats, 4g net carbs, and 63.8g protein.

Lunch recipes

Crispy curry rubbed chicken thigh

TIME TO PREPARE
10 minutes

COOK TIME
30 minutes

Serving
2 People

INGREDIENTS

- 2 chicken thighs
- 1 tbsp. Olive oil
- 1/2 tsp. Yellow curry
- 1/2 tsp. Salt
- 1/4 tsp. Cumin
- 1/4 tsp. Paprika
- 1/4 tsp. Garlic powder
- 1/8 tsp. Cayenne pepper
- 1/8 tsp. Allspice
- 1/8 tsp. Chili powder
- 1/8 tsp. Coriander
- Pinch cardamom
- Pinch cinnamon
- Pinch ginger

INSTRUCTIONS

1. Preheat oven to 425f.
2. Mix together all spices into a bowl.
3. Wrap a baking sheet in foil and lay chicken thighs on to the foil.
4. Rub olive oil evenly into all chicken thighs.
5. Rub spice mixture on both sides of the chicken, coating liberally.
6. Bake for 40-50 minutes.
7. Let cool for 5 minutes before serving.

Nutrition Per Serving: 555 calories, 39.8g fats, 1.3g net carbs, and 42.3g protein.

Lunch recipes

Greek Salad

TIME TO PREPARE
10 minutes

COOK TIME
5 minutes

Serving
2 People

INGREDIENTS

- One head iceberg lettuce—washed, cored and quartered
- 1-pint cherry tomatoes, quartered
- ½ cucumber, thinly sliced
- ½ red onion, thinly sliced
- ½ cup crumbled feta cheese
- 1 cup kalamata olives
- Four peperoncino peppers

INSTRUCTIONS

1. Place a quarter of iceberg lettuce on each plate and then sprinkle with an even amount of the tomatoes, cucumber, and red onion. Drizzle each wedge with salad dressing to taste.
2. Garnish with two tablespoons feta, ¼ cup olives, and a peperoncino pepper. Serve immediately.

Nutrition Per Serving: 153 calories, 8g fat, 18g carbs, 6g protein, 10g sugars,

Lunch recipes

Drunken five spice beef

TIME TO PREPARE
10 minutes

COOK TIME
25 minutes

Serving
4 People

INGREDIENTS

- 1 1/2 lbs. Ground beef
- 1 can coors light (or 1/2 cup red wine)
- 150g sliced mushrooms

- 135g chopped broccoli
- 75g raw spinach
- 3 tbsp. Reduced sugar ketchup
- 2 tbsp. Soy sauce
- 2 tsp. Garlic
- 2 tsp. Minced ginger
- 1 tbsp. Five spice
- 1 tbsp. Pepper
- 2 tsp. Salt
- 2 tsp. Cumin
- 1 tsp. Cayenne pepper
- 1/2 tsp. Onion powder

INSTRUCTIONS

1. Chop up broccoli florets, ginger, and garlic.
2. Bring cast iron to high heat and add ground beef.
3. Brown all ground beef then add ginger and garlic to the pan.
4. Mix everything well, add broccoli and spices and stir everything together.
5. Pour 1 can of coors light (or other low carb beer, or 1/2 cup red wine) into the pan. Add mushrooms and spinach and mix everything in together.
6. Once spinach has wilted, add ketchup, mix, and serve!

Nutrition Per Serving: 515 calories, 35g fats, 6g net carbs, and 33.3g protein.

Lunch recipes

Overnight Oats

TIME TO PREPARE
5 minutes

COOK TIME
5 minutes

Serving
2 People

INGREDIENTS

- 1 cup organic rolled oats
- 2 ½ cups Strawberry Cashew Milk
- 1 Tablespoon Chia seeds
- 1 Tablespoon Whole flax seeds

INSTRUCTIONS

1. Place rolled oats, chia seeds, and flax seeds in a large bowl. Poor in 2 ½ cups of strawberry cashew milk (or preferred dairy, nut or seed milk) and stir well to combine. Cover and store in the fridge for 1 hour or overnight.
2. Check consistency and add additional Strawberry Cashew Milk as desired. Portion into individual containers. Add fresh strawberries, cashews, chia seeds, flax seeds, or extra Strawberry Cashew Milk as toppings. Enjoy immediately or store in airtight containers for up to 5 days.

Nutrition Per Serving: Fat: 70g, Carbohydrates: 35g, Protein: 15g, Calories: 533

Lunch recipes

Cheesy Frittata Muffins

TIME TO PREPARE
5 minutes

COOK TIME
20 minutes

Serving
4 People

INGREDIENTS

- 8 Large Eggs
- 1/2 Cup Half n' Half
- 4 Oz. Bacon
- 1/2 Cup Cheddar Cheese
- 1 Tbsp. Butter
- 2 tsp. Dried Parsley
- 1/2 tsp. Pepper
- 1/4 tsp. Salt

INSTRUCTIONS

1. Preheat oven to 375 degrees
2. Mix eggs and half n' half in a bowl until almost scrambled, leaving streaks of egg white
3. Fold in the bacon, cheese, and spices. Add any other additional ingredients now
4. Grease a muffin tin with butter. This recipe makes about 8 frittata muffins.
5. Pour the mixture, filling each cup about 3/4 way.
6. Stick them in the oven for 15-18 minutes, or until puffy and golden on the edges.
7. Remove from the oven and let cool for 1 minute. These freeze well and can be heated individually.

Nutrition Per Serving: 205 Calories, 16.1g Fats, 1.3g Net Carbs, and 13.6g Protein.

Lunch recipes

Fried queso fresco

TIME TO PREPARE
5 minutes

COOK TIME
20 minutes

Serving
4 People

INGREDIENTS

- 1 lb. Queso fresco
- 1 tbsp. Coconut oil
- 1/2 tbsp. Olive oil

INSTRUCTIONS

1. Cut cheese into cubes, or thin rectangles.
2. Bring 1 tbsp. Coconut oil and 1/2 tbsp. Olive oil to high heat in a pan.
3. Once the smoke point hits, add your cheese. Let it cook until browned on one side and then flip over and do the same on the other side.
4. Remove from pan and drain excess grease on a paper towel.

Nutrition Per Serving: 243 calories, 19.5g fats, 0g net carbs, and 16g protein.

Lunch recipes

Strawberry Cashew Milk

TIME TO PREPARE
10 minutes

COOK TIME
10 minutes

Serving
4 People

INGREDIENTS

- 2 cups raw, unsalted cashews
- 1 pint of strawberries (2-2 ½ cups)

- 4 cups of filtered water
- Pinch of sea salt
- 1 T raw honey (optional)

INSTRUCTIONS

1. Using a high-speed blender, add cashews and water to the pitcher.
2. While cashews are soaking, wash strawberries, trim to tops, and slice in half.
3. Add strawberries, sea salt, and optional sweetener. Blend on high for 1 minute till full incorporated and smooth.
4. Store in an airtight container in the fridge for up to 7 days.

Nutrition Per Serving: Fat: 44g, Carbohydrates: 5g, Protein: 27g, Calories: 516

Lunch recipes

Lemon rosemary chicken

TIME TO PREPARE
15 minutes

COOK TIME
35 minutes

Serving
2 People

INGREDIENTS

- 3 1/2 skinless, boneless chicken
- 1 1/2 tsp. Minced garlic
- 1 1/2 tsp. Olive oil 1 lemon
- 1 1/2 tsp. Fresh thyme
- 3/4 tsp. Dried rosemary
- 1/2 tsp. Dried ground sage

INSTRUCTIONS

1. In a mortar, add your garlic and 1 tsp. Kosher salt
2. Grind the garlic and salt together with a pestle, creating a paste.
3. Slowly add your oil, grinding and mixing the paste into an aioli.
4. Once the aioli is finished, dry your chicken off and put it into a bag with the aioli. Coat the chicken well.
5. Marinate the chicken for anywhere from 2-10 hours.
6. Preheat your oven to 425f.
7. Slice 1 lemon thin and arrange the slices on the bottom of a baking pan.

8. Lay your chicken on top of the lemons.
9. Remove the thyme leaves from the stem and add your thyme, rosemary, sage, pepper, and remaining salt to the chicken.
10. Bake for 25-30 minutes, or until the juices run clear.
11. Remove the chicken from the pan and add all the pan drippings to a saucepan.
12. Bring the sauce to a boil while stirring well.
13. Turn the heat down to medium-low while continuing to stir the sauce. Let it reduce.
14. Spoon the sauce over the chicken, enjoy!

Nutrition Per Serving: 589 calories, 40.5g fats, 4.2g net carbs, and 47g protein.

Lunch recipes

Keto szechuan chicken

TIME TO PREPARE
5 minutes

COOK TIME
25 minutes

Serving
4 People

INGREDIENTS

- 1 1/2 lbs. Ground chicken
- 6 cups spinach
- 1/2 cup chicken stock
- 4 tbsp. Organic tomato paste
- 3 tbsp. Coconut oil
- 2 tbsp. Chili garlic paste
- 2 tbsp. Soy sauce
- 1 tbsp. + 1 tsp. Erythritol

- 1 tbsp. Red wine vinegar
- 2 tsp. Spicy brown mustard
- 2 tsp. Salt
- 2 tsp. Pepper
- 1 tsp. Red pepper flakes
- 1/2 tsp. Mrs. Dash table blend
- 1/2 tsp. Minced ginger

INSTRUCTIONS

1. Mix together tomato paste, soy sauce, chili garlic paste, brown mustard, and ginger in a ramekin.
2. On the stove, bring 3 tbsp. Coconut oil to medium-high temperature.
3. Cook the ground chicken with salt and pepper in the oil until it is cooked through. Break it up into small pieces.
4. Add 2/3 of your sauce to the mixture and mix it well.
5. Add your spinach to the chicken and let it wilt. Add salt, pepper, mrs. Dash seasoning, red pepper flakes.
6. Add the last 1/3 of your sauce, chicken stock, red wine vinegar, and erythritol. Mix the spinach and spices in well.

7. Turn the heat to low and cover the pan. Let this cook for about 10-15 minutes.

Nutrition Per Serving: 515 calories, 38.3g fats, 5.2g net carbs, and 63g protein.

Lunch recipes

Egg & Mackerel Breakfast Kick-Start

TIME TO PREPARE
10 minutes

COOK TIME
15 minutes

Serving
2 People

INGREDIENTS

- 4 large eggs.
- 8 oz can of mackerel in tomato sauce.
- ½ red onion (finely sliced).
- ¼ cup olive oil.
- 2 oz lettuce.
- 2 tbsp butter.
- Salt and pepper.

INSTRUCTIONS

1. Melt butter in a frying pan and cook the eggs to your preference.
2. On a serving plate, place lettuce and top with onion. Add the eggs and mackerel to the plate.
3. Drizzle olive oil over the lettuce and season with salt and pepper.

Nutrition Per Serving: Fat: 59g, Carbohydrates: 4.2g, Protein: 35g, Calories: 689,

Lunch recipes

Omnivore burger with creamed

TIME TO PREPARE
10 minutes

COOK TIME
20 minutes

Serving
2 People

INGREDIENTS

- 1-pound ground beef
- 100g sliced mushrooms
- 1/4 onion
- 1/4 bell pepper
- 2 1/2 cups raw spinach
- 2 1/2 tbsp. Roasted almonds
- 1 tbsp. Cream cheese
- 1/2 tbsp. Heavy cream
- 1/2 tbsp. Butter
- 1/2 tbsp. Tone's southwest chipotle seasoning
- 1 tsp. Cumin
- 1 tsp. Red pepper flakes

INSTRUCTIONS

1. Preheat oven to 450 convection or 475 normal.
2. Measure out 100g mushrooms, 1/4 onion, and 1/4 bell pepper. Put the in the food processor and pulse until you have diced vegetables.
3. Add your meat, diced vegetables, and seasonings into a mixing bowl and mix well.
4. Portion out 3 burger patties from the meat mix.
5. Rest the 3 patties on a cooling rack that sits over a baking sheet. The baking sheet should be covered in foil and salt added to it
6. Put small amount of remaining meat into pan and bring to sizzle.
7. Add spinach and let it wilt down with some salt, pepper, and red pepper flakes.
8. Add almonds, cream cheese, butter, and heavy cream and stir it well. Let this continue to cook down and stay warm.
9. Remove the burgers from the oven after 19-24 minutes. Keep your eye on these as once they start getting past rare temperature, they cook quickly.

Nutrition Per Serving: 562 calories, 38.5g fats, 4.8g net carbs, and 45.3g protein.

Lunch recipes

Bacon wrapped pork tenderloin

TIME TO PREPARE
10 minutes

COOK TIME
20 minutes

Serving
2 People

INGREDIENTS

- 1 lb. Pork tenderloin
- 2 slices bacon
- 2 tsp. Dijon mustard
- 2 tsp. Sugar free maple syrup
- 3/4 tsp. Soy sauce
- 1/4 tsp. Minced garlic
- 1/4 tsp. Liquid smoke
- 1/4 tsp. Dried rosemary
- Pinch black pepper
- Pinch cayenne
- Pinch dried sage

INSTRUCTIONS

1. Mix together all of the wet and dry ingredients to make the marinade.
2. Pat the pork tenderloins dry and add them to a ziploc bag.
3. Pour marinade into bag and rub onto the tenderloins. Put this in the fridge for 3-5 hours.
4. Preheat oven to 350f.
5. Put pork tenderloins on a foiled baking sheet, and wrap in bacon. About 5 slices per tenderloin.
6. Bake for 1 hour, then broil the bacon for 5-10 minutes.
7. Cover the tenderloins with foil for 10-15 minutes to rest. Cut and serve.

Nutrition Per Serving: 418 calories, 20g fats, 0.3g net carbs, and 54g protein.

Lunch recipes

Keto-Classic Cereal

TIME TO PREPARE
10 minutes

COOK TIME
15 minutes

Serving
4 People

INGREDIENTS

- 1 cup almond flour.
- 2 tbsp water.
- 2 tbsp sunflower seeds.
- 1 tbsp coconut oil.
- 1 tbsp flaxseed meal.
- 1 tsp vanilla extract.
- 1 tsp cinnamon (ground).
- ¼ tsp salt.

INSTRUCTIONS

1. Preheat oven at 350 degrees.
2. Add almond flour, sunflower seeds, flaxseed meal, cinnamon, and salt to a blender and blend until sunflower seeds are finely chopped.
3. Mix in the water and coconut oil and blend until a dough is formed.
4. Place dough on a piece of greaseproof paper and press flat. Place another piece of greaseproof paper on top and roll the dough until it is approximately 3mm in thickness.
5. Remove top paper and cut the dough into 1-inch squares.
6. Place the greaseproof paper (with the cut squares) on to a baking tray.
7. Bake in the oven for 10-15 minutes or until lightly browned and crisp.
8. Allow to cool and then separate the squares.
9. Serve with unsweetened almond milk.

Nutrition Per Serving: Fat: 18g, Carbohydrates: 3g, Protein: 6g, Calories: 207

Lunch recipes

Red pepper spinach salad

TIME TO PREPARE
5 minutes

COOK TIME
5 minutes

Serving
2 People

INGREDIENTS

3 cups spinach
2 tbsp. Ranch dressing
1 1/2 tbsp. Parmesan cheese
1/2 tsp. Red pepper flakes

INSTRUCTIONS

1. Add spinach to a mixing bowl, then drench in ranch.
2. Mix everything together and add your parmesan and red pepper flakes.
3. Mix everything together again and serve.

Nutrition Per Serving: 208 calories, 18g fats, 3.5g net carbs, and 8g protein.

Lunch recipes

The Magnificent Mushroom

TIME TO PREPARE
5 minutes

COOK TIME
10 minutes

Serving
2 People

INGREDIENTS

- 2 large deep cup mushrooms (stem removed).
- Four slices of bacon (cooked and chopped).
- Two large eggs.
- 1/10 cup parmesan (grated).

- Cooking spray.

INSTRUCTIONS

1. Preheat oven at 375 degrees.
2. On a baking tray, spray the mushrooms with cooking spray and bake for 10 minutes.
3. Split the bacon and parmesan between the two mushrooms and bake for an additional 5 minutes.
4. Crack an egg into each mushroom and bake for an additional 10 minutes.

Nutrition Per Serving: Fat: 47g, Carbohydrates: 8g, Protein: 30g, Calories: 578

Lunch recipes

Keto Crunchy Cauliflower Hash Browns

TIME TO PREPARE

10 minutes

COOK TIME

15 minutes

Serving

4 People

INGREDIENTS

- 16 oz cauliflower (head grated).
- Three large eggs.
- ½ onion (finely diced).
- 4 oz butter.
- 1 tsp salt.
- ¼ tsp black pepper.

INSTRUCTIONS

1. Add all ingredients (except butter) to a large bowl and mix until well combined. Allow standing for 10 minutes.
2. Melt ¼ butter in a large frying pan. Add two scoops of the cauliflower mixture; flatten carefully until they are 3-4 inches in diameter.
3. Fry for 4-5 minutes on each side.
4. Repeat until all the mixture has gone.

Nutrition Per Serving: Fat: 26g, Carbohydrates: 5g, Protein: 7g, Calories: 28

Lunch recipes

Baked Egg Breakfast Banquet

TIME TO PREPARE
5 minutes

COOK TIME
15 minutes

Serving
2 People

INGREDIENTS

- 2 large eggs.
- 3 oz minced beef.
- 2 oz cheddar cheese (grated).

INSTRUCTIONS

1. Preheat oven at 400 degrees.
2. Put the minced beef into a baking dish; make two holes in the mince and crack in the eggs.
3. Sprinkle the cheese over the top.
4. Bake for 10-15 minutes or until the eggs are cooked.

Nutrition Per Serving: Fat: 36g, Carbohydrates: 2g, Protein: 40g, Calories: 498

Lunch recipes

Classy Cheese & Onion Omelette

TIME TO PREPARE
10 minutes

COOK TIME
10 minutes

Serving
2 People

INGREDIENTS

- 4 large mushrooms.
- Three large eggs.
- ¼ onion (finely chopped).

- 1 oz cheddar cheese (grated).
- 1 oz butter.
- Salt and pepper.

INSTRUCTIONS

1. Whisk the eggs until smooth; add salt and pepper.
2. Over medium heat, melt the butter in a large frying pan. Add onion and mushrooms and cook until lightly browned and softened. Pour the egg mixture over the onions and mushrooms.
3. As the omelette is cooking and begins to firm, add the cheese.
4. Ease around the edges of the omelette with a spatula and fold in half.
5. Allow cooking until all is golden brown.

Nutrition Per Serving: Fat: 44g, Carbohydrates: 5g, Protein: 27g, Calories: 516

Dinner recipes

Shredded Fennel Salad with Chicken

TIME TO PREPARE
10 minutes

COOK TIME
15 minutes

Serving
4 People

INGREDIENTS

- 4 cups mixed salad greens or 5 oz container
- One fennel, fronds removed (1 cup shredded)
- ¼ red cabbage, shredded (1 cup shredded)
- 1/8 red onion (1/4 cup)
- ½ cup fresh herbs, such as mint, parsley, and cilantro
- Two chicken breasts
- 1 Tbsp Adobo Spice Mix
- Whipped Lemon Vinaigrette

INSTRUCTIONS

1. Preheat grill on high. Season chicken evenly with a spice mix. Grill on medium-high for 10 minutes, turning halfway through. Set aside to cool.
2. Prepare the salad by rough chopping mixed greens and place equally in two salad bowls. Using a mandolin, shave fennel bulb on the first or mini-setting of your mandolin, along with the red onion. If slicing with a knife, slice ¼ inch thin or thinner. Slice fennel shreds in half and toss with greens.

3. Shave the red cabbage on the other mandolin setting for ¼ inch slices. Mix with greens and fennel. Add fresh mint, parsley, dill, or cilantro. Lightly toss with Whipped Lemon Vinaigrette. Finish with sliced chicken breast. Garnish with avocado, feta, or goat cheese if desired. Holds well for meal prep for five days.

Nutrition Per Serving: Fat: 66g, Carbohydrates: 56g, Protein: 77g, Calories: 436

Dinner recipes

Roasted pecan green beans

TIME TO PREPARE
5 minutes

COOK TIME
20 minutes

Serving
2 People

INGREDIENTS

- 1/2-pound green beans
- 2 tbsp. Olive oil
- 1/4 cup chopped pecans
- 2 tbsp. Parmesan cheese
- 1/2 lemon's zest
- 1 tsp. Minced garlic
- 1/2 tsp. Red pepper flakes

INSTRUCTIONS

1. Preheat oven to 450f, then add pecans to your food processor.
2. Grind the pecans in the food processor until they are chopped Nicely. Some pieces should be large, some small.
3. In a large mixing bowl, mix together green beans, pecans, olive oil, parmesan cheese, the zest of 1/2 lemon, minced garlic, and red pepper flakes.
4. Spread out the green beans on a foiled baking sheet.
5. Roast the green beans in the oven for 20-25 minutes. 6. Let cool for 4-5 minutes, then serve!

Nutrition Per Serving: 182 calories, 16.8g fats, 3.3g net carbs, and 3.7g protein.

Dinner recipes

Shrimp & cauliflower curry

TIME TO PREPARE
15 minutes

COOK TIME
45 minutes

Serving
4 People

INGREDIENTS

24 oz. Shrimp
5 cups raw spinach
4 cups chicken stock
1 medium onion
1/2 head medium cauliflower
1 cup coconut milk
1/4 cup butter
1/4 cup heavy cream

3 tbsp. Olive oil
2 tbsp. Curry powder
1 tbsp. Coconut flour
1 tbsp. Cumin
2 tsp. Garlic powder
1 tsp. Chili powder
1 tsp. Onion powder
1 tsp. Cayenne

1 tsp. Paprika
1/2 tsp. Ground ginger
1/2 tsp. Coriander
1/2 tsp. Turmeric
1/4 tsp. Cardamom
1/4 tsp. Cinnamon
1/4 tsp. Xanthan gum

INSTRUCTIONS

1. Mix all spices (except xanthan and coconut flour), set aside.
2. Cut 1 medium onion into slices.
3. Bring 3 tbsp. Olive oil to hot heat in a pan. Add onion, cook onion till soft.
4. Add butter, heavy cream 1/8 tsp. Xanthan and spices, stir it in so it's all mixed well.
5. After about 1-2 mins of the spices sweating, add 4 cups chicken broth, and 1 cup coconut milk. Stir well and cover.
6. Cook for 30 mins, with the lid on. Chop cauliflower into small florets then add to curry. Cook for another 15 minutes, covered.
7. Detail and devein shrimp, then add them to the curry. Cook for an additional 20 minutes with the lid off.
8. Measure out coconut flour and 1/8 tsp. Xanthan gum and stir well into curry. Let cook for 5 minutes.
9. After 5 minutes, add spinach and mix it in well. Cook for an addition 5-10 minutes with the lid off.

Nutrition Per Serving: 331 calories, 19.5g fats, 5.6g net carbs, and 27.4g protein.

Dinner recipes

Paleo Lamb Meatballs

TIME TO PREPARE
10 minutes

COOK TIME
15 minutes

Serving
2 People

INGREDIENTS

- 1-lb ground lamb
- One egg
- 2 tsp Organic Italian spice blend
- 1 tsp cumin powder
- 1 tsp coriander powder
- 3 tsp dried oregano
- 3 tsp whole fennel seeds
- 1 Tbsp fresh parsley, generous amount, minced
- ¼ tsp sea salt
- ¼ tsp coarse black pepper

INSTRUCTIONS

1. Preheat oven to 400 degrees. Prepare a baking pan with parchment paper.
2. In a medium bowl, combine lamb, egg, and spices blend well with your hands. Separate and roll into four even balls. Say a positive affirmation or word while forming the meatballs.
3. Place on the baking sheet and bake for 20 minutes. Enjoy immediately or store in an airtight container for up to 5 days.

Nutrition Per Serving: Fat: 24g, Carbohydrates: 77g, Protein: 135g, Calories: 485

Dinner recipes

Simple lunch salad

TIME TO PREPARE
5 minutes

COOK TIME
2 minutes

Serving
4 People

INGREDIENTS

4 tbsp. Olive oil
2 cups spinach
2 tbsp. Parmesan cheese
1 1/2 tsp. Dijon mustard
3/4 tsp. Curry powder
1/4 lemon meat specified in day-by-day

INSTRUCTIONS

1. Combine all wet ingredients in a small bowl.
2. Combine meat and spinach in a bowl.
3. Pour wet ingredients over meat and spinach when ready to eat.

Nutrition Per Serving: 18 calories, 20g fats, 0.3g net carbs, and 54g protein.

Dinner recipes

Carob Avocado Mousse

TIME TO PREPARE
10 minutes

COOK TIME
10 minutes

Serving
4 People

INGREDIENTS

- 2 Ripe bananas
- 2 Ripe avocados
- 2/3 Carob powder
- 3 T Maple syrup

- 1 tsp Vanilla extract
- 1/8 tsp Stevia (or to taste)

INSTRUCTIONS

1. Using a small bowl, peel the banana and break into pieces. Smash well with a fork or potato masher. Add the avocados and do the same. Mix well till banana and avocado are incorporated. For a smoother mousse texture, purée the mash with a hand blender or small food processor until smooth.
2. Add in the carob powder slowly, in three parts, and combine well.
3. Add maple syrup and continue to blend.
4. Taste test, and add 1/8 teaspoon of stevia for additional sweetness to taste.
5. Transfer the mousse to individual bowls and serve. Store in the fridge until ready to eat, up to five days. Keeps well in the freezer for six months.

Nutrition Per Serving: Fat: 39g, Carbohydrates: 365g, Protein: 965g, Calories: 55g

Dinner recipes

Chicken and bacon sausage stir fry

TIME TO PREPARE
5 minutes

COOK TIME
15 minutes

Serving
2 People

INGREDIENTS

- 4 chicken sausages
- 3 cups broccoli florets
- 3 cups spinach
- 1/2 cup parmesan cheese
- 1/2 cup rao's tomato sauce
- 1/4 cup red wine
- 2 tbsp. Salted butter
- 2 tsp. Minced garlic
- 1/2 tsp. Red pepper flakes

INSTRUCTIONS

1. Slice the 4 bacon & cheddar chicken sausages.
2. Start to boil water on the stove. While that is happening, add your sausage to a pan on high heat.

3. Add your broccoli to the boiling water and cook for 3-5 minutes depending on how you like it done.
4. Stir your sausages until they brown on both sides.
5. Move your sausages to one side of the pan, then add the butter. Put your garlic in the butter and let it saute for 1 minute.
6. Mix everything together and then add your broccoli.
7. Pour in the tomato sauce, red wine, and add red pepper flakes.
8. Mix together, add your spinach with salt and pepper and let it cook down. Simmer this for 5-10 minutes.

Nutrition Per Serving: 451 calories, 28.3g fats, 7.3g net carbs, and 35.7g protein.

Dinner recipes

Taco tartlets

TIME TO PREPARE
10 minutes

COOK TIME
30 minutes

Serving
6 People

INGREDIENTS

The pastry

- 1 cup blanched almond flour
- 3 tbsp. Coconut flour
- 5 tbsp. Butter
- 1/4 tsp. Salt
- 1 tsp. Xanthan gum
- 1 tsp. Oregano
- 1/4 tsp. Paprika

- 1/4 tsp. Cayenne
- 2 tbsp. Ice water

The filling

- 1/3 cup cheese
- 400g ground beef
- 80g mushroom
- 3 stalks spring onion
- 2 tbsp. Tomato paste

- 1 tbsp. Olive oil
- 2 tsp. Yellow mustard
- 2 tsp. Garlic 1 tsp. Cumin
- 1/2 tsp. Pepper
- 1 tsp. Salt 1 tsp. Worcestershire
- 1/4 tsp. Cinnamon

INSTRUCTIONS

1. Combine all the dry ingredients of the pastry and put them into a food processor.
2. Chop cold butter into small squares and add it to your food processor also. Pulse the dough together until crumbly, adding 1 tbsp. Ice water until pliable.
3. Chill your dough in the freezer for 10 minutes.
4. Roll the dough out between 2 silpats using a rolling pin. Cut out circles using a cookie cutter or a glass.

5. Put the dough into your whoopie pan and preheat your oven to 325f.
6. Prep all the filling ingredients – chop spring onions, mince garlic, and slice mushrooms.
7. Saute onions and garlic in olive oil. Add ground beef to the mixture and sear it well – adding dry spices and worcestershire.
8. Add mushrooms and mix together. Then add tomato paste and
9. Mustard right before finishing.
10. Spoon ground beef mixture evenly into the pastry tartlets. Cover with cheese and bake for 20-25 minutes.

Nutrition Per Serving: 241 calories, 19.4g fats, 1.7g net carbs, and 13.1g protein.

Dinner recipes

Egg & Bacon Sandwich

TIME TO PREPARE
5 minutes

COOK TIME
10 minutes

Serving
2 People

INGREDIENTS

- Cooking spray.
- Two large eggs.
- 1 tbsp coconut flour.
- 1 tbsp butter (salted).
- ¼ tsp baking powder.
- One slice cheddar cheese.
- Two slices of bacon (grilled)

INSTRUCTIONS

1. Place butter in the microwave for 30 seconds or until melted.
2. Let the butter cool slightly. Mix in 1 egg, coconut flour, and baking powder; microwave for one and a half minutes.
3. Allow bread to cool and slice to make two equally thin slices.
4. Using the cooking spray, fry the remaining egg to your preference. Grill the bread until toasted and crunchy.
5. Assemble the sandwich placing a slice of toast on the bottom, cheese, bacon, and fried egg; top with remaining toast.

Nutrition Per Serving: Fat: 39g, Carbohydrates: 6g, Protein: 28g, Calories: 490

Dinner recipes

Thai peanut chicken

TIME TO PREPARE
10 minutes

COOK TIME
20 minutes

Serving
2 People

INGREDIENTS

- 6 boneless, skinless chicken thighs
- 1 cup peanuts
- 1/4 cup chicken stock
- 2 tbsp. Soy sauce
- 1 tbsp. Orange juice
- 1 tbsp. Lemon juice
- 1 tbsp. Rice vinegar
- 1/2 tbsp. Coconut oil
- 1/2 tbsp. Erythritol
- 1/2 tsp. Sesame oil
- 2 tsp. Chili garlic paste
- 1/4 tsp. Coriander
- 1/4 tsp. Cayenne pepper
- Salt + pepper to taste

INSTRUCTIONS

1. Rinse peanuts off and spin them in a salad spinner to get rid of extra moisture. Pat dry with paper towels.
2. Put the nuts in your food processor and blend until creamy. Add coconut oil and erythritol and blend further.
3. Mix together all of the ingredients except for salt and pepper to make the sauce.
4. Cube your chicken thighs and season with salt and pepper.
5. Heat 1 tbsp. Olive oil to high heat in a pan. Add your chicken once hot.
6. Pat the extra moisture out of the pan with a paper towel. Continue cooking until chicken is browned on both sides.
7. Stir in your peanut butter sauce and add 1/4 tsp. Cayenne pepper and more salt and pepper if you wish.
8. Turn to low and let simmer for 10 minutes.

Nutrition Per Serving: 743 calories, 53.5g fats, 8.8g net carbs, and 70.5g protein.

Dinner recipes

Vegetable medley

TIME TO PREPARE
5 minutes

COOK TIME
10 minutes

Serving
4 People

INGREDIENTS

- 6 tbsp. Olive oil
- 240g baby bella mushrooms
- 115g broccoli
- 100g sugar snap peas
- 90g bell pepper
- 90g spinach
- 2 tbsp. Pumpkin seeds
- 2 tsp. Minced garlic
- 1 tsp. Salt
- 1 tsp. Pepper
- 1/2 tsp. Red pepper flakes

INSTRUCTIONS

1. Prep all vegetables by chopping them into small, bite size pieces.
2. Heat oil in a pan to high heat. Once hot, add garlic and let saute for 1 minute.
3. Add mushrooms and let them soak up some of the oil. Once they do, add broccoli and mix together well.
4. Let broccoli cook for a few minutes, then add sugar snap peas. Mix this together well.
5. Add bell pepper, spices, and pumpkin seeds then mix together well.
6. Once everything is cooked, lay spinach on top of the vegetables and let the steam wilt it.
7. Once the spinach wilts, mix it all together and serve

Nutrition Per Serving: 330 calories, 30.7g fats, 7.7g net carbs, and 6.7g protein.

Dinner recipes

Keto-Buzz Blueberry Pancakes

TIME TO PREPARE
10 minutes

COOK TIME
20 minutes

Serving
2 People

INGREDIENTS

- Three large eggs.
- ½ cup almond flour.
- ¼ cup of milk.
- ¼ cup of fresh blueberries.
- 2 tbsp coconut flour.
- 2 tbsp sweetener (granulated).
- 1 tsp cinnamon (ground).
- ½ tsp baking powder.

INSTRUCTIONS

1. Add all ingredients (except blueberries) to a blender and mix until a thick batter is formed.
2. Add the blended mixture to a bowl and stir in blueberries.
3. Grease a large non-stick frying pan and allow the pot to get hot over medium heat.
4. Pour ¼ cup of the mixture into the hot pan, allow to cook for 2 - 3 minutes, or until the edges start to crisp and turn lightly browned. Flip and repeat.
5. Repeat the process using the remaining batter.

Nutrition Per Serving: Fat: 7g, Carbohydrates: 4g, Protein: 7g, Calories: 132

Dinner recipes

Bacon Infused Sugar Snap Peas

TIME TO PREPARE
5 minutes

COOK TIME
10 minutes

Serving
4 People

INGREDIENTS

- 1 1/2 lb. Ground Beef
- 4 Slices Bacon
- 1 Cup Mozzarella Cheese
- 3/4 Cup Pesto Sauce
- 1/3 Cup Crushed Pork Rinds
- 2 Large Eggs
- 1 tsp. Pepper
- 2 tsp. Minced Garlic
- 1/2 tsp. Onion Powder
- 1/2 tsp. Kosher Salt

INSTRUCTIONS

1. Preheat oven to 350F.
2. Slice your bacon into small pieces (almost into small cubes).
3. Add your ground beef, ground pork rinds, spices, cheese, and eggs to the bacon.
4. Mix everything together well until you can form meatballs.
5. Roll your meatballs out into circles and place them in a foiled baking tray.
6. Bake in the oven for 40-45 minutes, or until bacon is cooked.
7. Spoon out 1/2 Tbsp. Pesto sauce per meatball and serve.

Nutrition Per Serving: 128 Calories, 9.4g Fats, 0.7g Net Carbs, and 10.1g Protein.

Dinner recipes

Inside Out Bacon Burger

TIME TO PREPARE
10 minutes

COOK TIME
15 minutes

Serving
2 People

INGREDIENTS

- 200g Ground Beef
- 2 Slices Bacon
- 2 Tbsp. Cheddar Cheese
- 1 1/2 tsp. Chopped Chives
- 1/2 tsp. Minced Garlic

- 1/2 tsp. Black Pepper
- 3/4 tsp. Soy Sauce
- 1/2 tsp. Salt
- 1/4 tsp. Onion Powder
- 1/4 tsp. Worcestershire

INSTRUCTIONS

7. In a cast iron skillet, cook all your chopped bacon until crisp. Once cooked, remove and place on paper towel. Drain grease separately and save.
8. In a large mixing bowl, combine ground beef, 2/3 chopped bacon, and the rest of the spices.
9. Mix meat and spices together well, then form into 3 patties.
10. Put 2 Tbsp. Bacon fat into cast iron and place patties inside once fat is hot.
11. Cook about 4-5 minutes on each side, depending on the done-ness you want.
12. Remove from pan, let rest for 3-5 minutes, and serve with cheese, extra bacon, and onion if you'd like.

Nutrition Per Serving: 649 Calories, 51.8g Fats, 1.8g Net Carbs, and 43.5g Protein.

Dinner recipes

Mozzarella Pockets of Pleasure

TIME TO PREPARE
5 minutes

COOK TIME
15 minutes

Serving
4 People

INGREDIENTS

- 3 eggs.
- 8 oz mozzarella (grated).
- 4 oz bacon (grilled).
- 2 oz cream cheese.
- ⅔ cup almond flour.
- ½ cup cheddar cheese (grated).
- ⅓ cup coconut flour.
- 2 tsp baking powder.
- 1 tsp salt.

INSTRUCTIONS

1. Preheat oven at 350 degrees.
2. Microwave the cream cheese and mozzarella for 60 seconds. Stir and microwave for an additional 60 seconds.
3. Put one egg, almond flour, coconut flour, baking powder, and salt into a blender and pour in the melted cheese mixture. Blend until a dough forms.
4. Split the dough into eight pieces. Flatten each piece to form a 5-inch circle, place on a baking tray lined with baking paper.
5. Scramble the remaining two eggs and divide between each circle; do the same with bacon and cheddar cheese.
6. Fold the edges in and seal the semi-circle using fingertips.
7. Bake for 20 minutes or until lightly browned.

Nutrition Per Serving: Fat:18g, Carbohydrates: 6.5g, Protein: 16g, Calories: 258

Dinner recipes

What Waffle!

TIME TO PREPARE
10 minutes

COOK TIME
15 minutes

Serving
4 People

INGREDIENTS

- 2 large eggs.
- 2 cups almond flour.
- 1 ½ cups almond milk (warm).
- ⅓ cup butter (melted).
- 2 tbsp erythritol.
- 4 tsp baking powder.
- 1 tsp vanilla extract.
- 1 tsp salt.

INSTRUCTIONS

1. Mix baking powder, salt, and almond flour until well combined.
2. In a separate bowl, whisk the eggs until well combined.
3. Take the lukewarm almond milk and mix with the eggs, adding melted butter, erythritol, and vanilla extract.
4. Stir the egg mixture into the flour mixture until a dough is formed. Let sit for several minutes.
5. Cook in a hot waffle iron for 6-8 minutes.

Nutrition Per Serving: Fat: 31g, Carbohydrates: 8g, Protein: 11g, Calories: 345

Dinner recipes

Bacon & Egg Pick-me-up

TIME TO PREPARE
5 minutes

COOK TIME
10 minutes

Serving
4 People

INGREDIENTS

- 8 large eggs.
- 5 oz bacon (slices).
- A handful of cherry tomatoes (halved).

INSTRUCTIONS

1. In a large frying pan, fry bacon rashers until crispy. Set aside, leaving bacon fat in the pan.
2. Crack the eggs into the frying pan and fry eggs to your preferred taste.
3. When eggs are nearly cooked, throw in the cherry tomatoes and fry until lightly browned.

Nutrition Per Serving: Fat: 24g, Carbohydrates: 1g, Protein: 17g, Calories: 274

Dinner recipes

No-Fuss Egg Medley Muffins

TIME TO PREPARE
10 minutes

COOK TIME
15 minutes

Serving
4 People

INGREDIENTS

- 12 large eggs.
- One onion (finely chopped).
- 6 oz cheddar cheese (grated).
- 5 oz bacon (cooked and diced).

- Pinch salt and pepper.

INSTRUCTIONS

1. Preheat the oven at 175 degrees and grease a 12-hole muffin tray.
2. Equally, place onion and bacon to the bottom of each muffin tray hole.
3. In a large bowl, whisk the eggs, cheese, salt, and pepper.
4. Pour the egg mixture into each hole; on top of the onions and bacon.
5. Bake for 15-20 minutes, until browned and firm to the touch.

Nutrition Per Serving: Fat: 28g, Carbohydrates: 2g, Protein: 22g, Calories: 333

Dinner recipes

Charming Cream Cheese Breakfast Pancakes

TIME TO PREPARE
5 minutes

COOK TIME
10 minutes

Serving
2 People

INGREDIENTS

- 4 large eggs
- 2 oz cream cheese.
- 4 tsp granulated sugar substitute.
- 1 tsp ground cinnamon.

INSTRUCTIONS

1. Blend all ingredients until smooth. Allow resting for 2 minutes.
2. Grease a large frying pan and pour in ¼ of the mixture.
3. Cook for 2 minutes until golden, flip and cook for an additional minute.
4. Repeat the process until all mixture has gone.

Nutrition Per Serving: Fat: 30g, Carbohydrates: 3g, Protein: 16g, Calories: 346

Dinner recipes

Keto Chocolate Hazelnut Muffins

TIME TO PREPARE
10 minutes

COOK TIME
20 minutes

Serving
12 People

INGREDIENTS

- 3 cups of almond flour (360 g)
- 1/2 cup of coconut oil (120 ml),
- 1/2 cup of hazelnuts (100 g), chopped
- 4 large eggs, whisked
- 1/2 teaspoon of ground nutmeg (1 g)
- 1/4 teaspoon of ground cloves (1 g)
- Stevia or low carb sweetener of choice, to taste
- Dash of salt
- 1 teaspoon of baking soda (8 g)
- 3 oz of 100% dark chocolate (80 g), broken into small piece

INSTRUCTIONS

1. Preheat oven to 350 F (175 C). Grease a 12-cup muffin pan with coconut oil or line with paper liners.
2. In a large bowl, mix to combine the almond flour, melted coconut oil, chopped hazelnuts, whisked eggs, ground nutmeg, ground cloves, stevia, salt, and baking soda.
3. Pour equal amounts of batter into the prepared muffin pan. Place equal amounts of the dark chocolate pieces into each muffin cup. Press the chocolate pieces into the batter.
4. Place the muffin pan in the oven and bake for 18 to 20 minutes until a toothpick comes out clean when inserted into a muffin.
5. Remove the muffin pan from the oven and let cool before serving. Store any leftover muffins in an airtight container

Nutrition Per Serving: Calories: 282 Fat: 25 g Fiber: 3 g Sugar: 1 g Net Carbs: 3 g Protein: 8 g

Dinner recipes

Keto Bacon Mini Frittata

TIME TO PREPARE
10 minutes

COOK TIME
30 minutes

Serving
4 People

INGREDIENTS

- Avocado oil, to grease a muffin pan
- 4 slices of bacon (112 g), diced
- 8 spears of asparagus (128 g), chopped small
- 2 Tablespoons chopped onions (30 g)
- 8 medium eggs, whisked
- 1/2 cup of coconut milk (120 ml)
- Salt and pepper, to taste

INSTRUCTIONS

1. Preheat oven to 350 F (175 C). Grease a 12-cup muffin pan with avocado oil or line with paper liners.
2. In a medium skillet, saute the bacon over medium-high heat until crispy, about 5 minutes. Remove the bacon from the skillet with a slotted spoon and drain on a paper towel-lined plate.
3. In a medium bowl, combine the cooked bacon, asparagus, and chopped onions with the eggs and coconut milk. Season with salt, to taste. Pour equal amounts of the egg mixture into the prepared muffin pan.
4. Place the muffin pan in the oven and bake for 25 to 30 minutes until the eggs are set but still slightly soft. Refrigerate any leftover muffins in an airtight container.

Nutrition Per Serving: Calories: 460 Fat: 41 g Fiber: 1 g Sugar: 2 g Net Carbs: 3 g Protein: 19 g

Dinner recipes

Bacon and Avocado Caesar Salad

TIME TO PREPARE
10 minutes

COOK TIME
5 minutes

Serving
2 People

INGREDIENTS

For the salad

- 4 slices of bacon (112 g), diced
- 1 head of romaine lettuce (200 g), chopped
- 1/2 cucumber (110 g), thinly sliced
- 1/4 medium onion (28 g), thinly sliced
- 1 large avocado (200 g), sliced

For the Caesar dressing

- 1/2 cup of mayo (120 ml)
- 2 Tablespoons of lemon juice (30 ml)
- 2 teaspoons of Dijon mustard (10 ml)
- 2 teaspoons of garlic powder (7 g)
- Salt and pepper, to taste

INSTRUCTIONS

1. Add the bacon to a large nonstick skillet over medium-high heat and saute until crispy, about 5 minutes. Remove the bacon from the skillet with a slotted spoon and place on a paper towel-lined plate to cool.
2. In a large bowl, whisk to combine the mayo, lemon juice, mustard, and garlic powder. Season with salt and pepper, to taste. Refrigerate half of the Caesar dressing in an airtight container for Day 6 Lunch (L6).
3. Toss the remaining Caesar dressing with the romaine lettuce leaves. Add the cucumber and onion to the bowl and toss to combine.
4. Divide the salad between 2 plates and top each salad with equal amounts of cooked bacon and sliced avocado.

Nutrition Per Serving: Calories: 652 Fat: 65 g Fiber: 9 g Sugar: 3 g Net Carbs: 6 g Protein: 10 g

Bonus recipes

Vanilla latte cookies

TIME TO PREPARE
10 minutes

COOK TIME
15 minutes

Serving
6 People

INGREDIENTS

1 1/2 cups honeyville blanched almond flour
1/2 cup unsalted butter
1/3 cup now erythritol
2 large eggs
1 tbsp. + 1 tsp. Instant coffee grounds
1 1/2 tsp. Vanilla extract
1/2 tsp. Baking soda
1/2 tsp. Kosher salt
1/4 tsp. Cinnamon
17 drops liquid stevia

INSTRUCTIONS

1. Preheat your oven to 350f.
2. In a mixing bowl, combine your almond flour, coffee grounds, baking soda, salt, and cinnamon.
3. In separate containers or bowls, separate your egg whites and egg yolks.
4. In another mixing bowl, add your butter and beat it well. Add your erythritol to the butter and continue beating it until almost white in color.
5. Add your egg yolks to the butter and mix until smooth.
6. Add half of the mixed almond flour to the butter and mix it in. Add your vanilla extract and liquid stevia, then add the rest of your almond flour and mix well.
7. Beat your egg whites until stiff peaks form. Fold the egg whites into the cookie dough.
8. Divide your cookies on a cookie sheet, i made 10 large cookies. Bake them for 12-15 minutes.
9. Once finished, remove the cookies to a cooling rack for 10-15 minutes.

Nutrition Per Serving: 167 calories, 17.1g fats, 1.4g net carbs, and 3.9g protein.

Bonus recipes

Lemon Pepper Tuna Salad

TIME TO PREPARE
10 minutes

COOK TIME
5 minutes

Serving
2 People

INGREDIENTS

- 2 cans of tuna (340 g), drained and flaked
- 2 Tablespoons of mayo (30 ml)
- 1 Tablespoon of Dijon mustard (15 ml)
- 2 teaspoons of lemon juice (10 ml) (or to taste)
- 4 cups of spinach (120 g)
- 2 Tablespoons of olive oil (30 ml)
- 1 large avocado (200 g), sliced
- Dash of pepper

INSTRUCTIONS

1. In a medium bowl, combine the tuna with the mayo, mustard, and lemon juice. Season with pepper, to taste.
2. In a large bowl, toss the spinach with the olive oil. Divide the spinach between 2 plates.
3. Divide the tuna salad in 2 and place on top of the spinach. Top the tuna salad with equal amounts of sliced avocado and serve

Nutrition Per Serving:
Calories: 614 Fat: 46 g Total Carbs: 11 g Fiber: 9 g Sugar: 1 g Net Carbs: 2 g Protein: 45 g

Bonus recipes

Bbq pulled chicken

TIME TO PREPARE
10 minutes

COOK TIME
35 minutes

Serving
4 People

INGREDIENTS

- 6 boneless, skinless chicken thighs
- 1/3 cup salted butter
- 1/4 cup erythritol
- 1/4 cup red wine vinegar
- 1/4 cup chicken stock
- 1/4 cup organic tomato paste
- 2 tbsp. Yellow mustard
- 2 tbsp. Spicy brown mustard
- 1 tbsp. Liquid smoke
- 1 tbsp. Soy sauce
- 2 tsp. Chili powder
- 1 tsp. Cumin
- 1 tsp. Cayenne pepper
- 1 tsp. Red boat fish sauce

INSTRUCTIONS

1. Mix together all ingredients except for butter and chicken thighs.
2. Place frozen (or fresh) chicken thighs in slow cooker and pour sauce over them.
3. If you aren't going to be home, add butter, turn to low and leave for 7-10 hours.
4. If you are going to be home, let cook on low for 2 hours.
5. Add your butter, turn to high, and cook for an additional 3 hours.
6. Once your chicken has cooked down, shred the chicken with 2 forks.
7. Mix all the sauce together and let cook on high for 45 minutes without the top. This will reduce the sauce.
8. Serve with coarse sea salt sprinkled over the top, along with chili paste and a sprinkle of curry powder for color.

Nutrition Per Serving: 510 calories, 30g fats, 2.3g net carbs, and 51.5g protein.

Bonus recipes

Quick Ground Beef Stir-Fry

TIME TO PREPARE
10 minutes

COOK TIME
15 minutes

Serving
2 People

INGREDIENTS

- 2 Tablespoons of coconut oil (30 ml), to cook with
- 2 medium bell peppers (240 g), sliced
- 10 cherry tomatoes (170 g), chopped
- 1/2 medium onion (55 g), thinly sliced
- 3/4 lb of ground beef (338 g)
- 2 cloves of garlic (6 g), minced or finely diced
- 1 teaspoon of hot sauce (5 ml) (or to taste) (optional)
- 2 Tablespoons of fresh cilantro (2 g), chopped
- Salt and pepper, to taste

INSTRUCTIONS

1. In a large skillet, melt the coconut oil over medium-high heat. Add the bell peppers, tomatoes, and onion to the skillet and stir-fry until slightly soft, about 5 minutes.
2. Add the ground beef to the skillet and stir-fry until browned, about 1 to 3 minutes.
3. Add the garlic, optional hot sauce, and fresh cilantro to the skillet and continue to stir-fry until the ground beef is cooked to your liking, about an additional 2 to 5 minutes. Season with salt and pepper, to taste.
4. Divide the stir-fry between 2 plates and serve.

Nutrition Per Serving: Calories: 620 Fat: 50 g Total Carbs: 13 g Fiber: 4 g Sugar: 6 g Net Carbs: 9 g Protein: 30 g

Bonus recipes

Pan-Fried Tuscan Chicken "Pasta"

TIME TO PREPARE
10 minutes

COOK TIME
15 minutes

Serving
2 People

INGREDIENTS

- 2 medium eggs, whisked
- 2 teaspoons of garlic powder
- 2 teaspoons of Italian seasoning
- 1/4 teaspoon of salt
- Dash of pepper
- 2 chicken breasts
- 2 Tablespoons of avocado oil
- 14 cherry tomatoes
- 1/4 cup of fresh basil leaves chopped
- 1 zucchini (120 g), spiralized
- 1 Tablespoon of olive oil
- 1 teaspoon of lemon juice

INSTRUCTIONS

1. In a medium bowl, combine the eggs, garlic powder, Italian seasoning, salt, and pepper. Add the chicken to the bowl and combine until the chicken is completely covered with the egg mixture.
2. Add the avocado oil to a large skillet over medium-high heat. Add the chicken to the skillet and saute until cooked through, about 6 to 8 minutes.
3. Add the tomatoes and fresh basil to the skillet and saute until the tomatoes are soft, about 2 to 3 minutes. Season with salt and pepper, to taste.
4. Meanwhile, in a separate bowl, toss the zucchini "pasta" with the olive oil and lemon juice.
5. Divide the zucchini "pasta" between 2 plates. Top the "pasta" with equal amounts of the chicken and serve.

Nutrition Per Serving:
Calories: 671 Fat: 45 g Total Carbs: 8 g Fiber: 2 g Sugar: 5 g Net Carbs: 6 g Protein: 54 g

Bonus recipes

Bulletproof coffee

TIME TO PREPARE
5 minutes

COOK TIME
5 minutes

Serving
2 People

INGREDIENTS

- 2 cup coffee
- 2 tbsp. Unsalted butter
- 2 tbsp. Coconut oil
- 2 tbsp. Heavy cream

INSTRUCTIONS

1. Brew a cup worth of coffee into a large container. I use a measuring cup.
2. Cut off 1 tbsp. Of butter. Drop your butter into the coffee and watch it ooze.
3. Measure out 1 tbsp. Of coconut oil and plunk that it into your coffee
4. Also.
5. Last but not least, the 1 tbsp. Of heavy cream. This adds a great creaminess to the coffee.
6. Mix it all together very well using a hand blender.

Nutrition Per Serving: 273 calories 30g fats, 1g net carbs, and 0g protein.

Bonus recipes

Chai spice mug cake

TIME TO PREPARE
5 minutes

COOK TIME
15 minutes

Serving
2 People

INGREDIENTS

Base

- 2 large egg
- 3 tbsp. Butter

- 3 tbsp. Honeyville almond flour
- 2 tbsp. Now erythritol
- 12 drops liquid stevia
- 2 tsp. Baking powder

Flavor

- 4 tbsp. Honeyville almond flour
- 1 tsp. Cinnamon
- 1 tsp. Ginger
- 1 tsp. Clove
- 1 tsp. Cardamom
- 1 tsp. Vanilla extract

INSTRUCTIONS

1. Mix all room temperature ingredients together in a mug.
2. Microwave on high for 70 seconds.
3. Turn cup upside down and lightly bang it against a plate.
4. Optional: top with whipped cream and sprinkle of cinnamon.

Nutrition Per Serving: 439 calories, 42g fats, 4g net carbs, and 12g protein.

Bonus recipes

Garlic Shrimp Caesar Salad

TIME TO PREPARE
10 minutes

COOK TIME
5 minutes

Serving
2 People

INGREDIENTS

- 2 Tablespoons of olive oil (30 ml), to cook with
- 1 lb of shrimp (450 g), defrosted if frozen, peeled and deveined
- 1 teaspoon of garlic powder (3 g)
- 1/2 teaspoon of onion powder (1 g)
- Leftover Caesar dressing from Day 1 Lunch (L1)
- 1 head of romaine lettuce (200 g), chopped
- 1/2 cucumber (110 g), thinly sliced
- Salt and pepper, to taste

INSTRUCTIONS

1. Add the olive oil to a large skillet over medium-high heat. Add the shrimp, garlic powder, and onion powder to the skillet and saute until the shrimp are cooked through and opaque, about 2 to 5 minutes. Season with salt and pepper, to taste,
2. In a large bowl, toss the leftover Caesar dressing with the romaine lettuce and sliced cucumber.
3. Divide the salad between 2 plates. Top each plate with equal amounts of shrimp and enjoy.

Nutrition Per Serving: Calories: 582 Fat: 43 g Total Carbs: 6 g Fiber: 2 g Sugar: 3 g Net Carbs: 4 g Protein: 47 g

Bonus recipes

Grilled Ribeyes with Greek Relish

TIME TO PREPARE
10 minutes

COOK TIME
15 minutes

Serving
4 People

INGREDIENTS

- Four plum tomatoes, seeded and chopped
- 1 cup chopped red onion
- 2/3 cup pitted Greek olives
- 1/4 cup minced fresh cilantro
- 1/4 cup lemon juice, divided
- Two tablespoons olive oil
- Two garlic cloves, minced
- Two beef ribeye steaks (3/4 pound each)
- 1 cup crumbled feta cheese

INSTRUCTIONS

1. For relish, combine tomatoes, onion, olives, cilantro, two tablespoons lemon juice, oil, and garlic.
2. Drizzle remaining lemon juice over steaks. Grill steaks, covered, over medium heat or broil 4 in. From heat 5-7 minutes on each side or until meat reaches desired doneness (for medium-rare, a thermometer should read 135°; medium, 140°; medium-well, 145°). Let stand 5 minutes before cutting steaks in half. Serve with relish and cheese.

Nutrition Per Serving: 597 calories, 44g fat, 115mg cholesterol,723mg sodium,11g carbohydrate,37g protein.

Bonus recipes

Chicken Salad

TIME TO PREPARE
5 minutes

COOK TIME
10 minutes

Serving
4 People

INGREDIENTS

- 1/2 cup mayonnaise
- 3 to 4 tablespoons barbecue sauce
- Two tablespoons finely chopped onion
- One tablespoon lemon juice
- 1/4 teaspoon pepper
- 8 cups torn salad greens
- Two large tomatoes, chopped
- 1-1/2 pounds boneless skinless chicken breasts, cooked and cubed
- Ten bacon strips, cooked and crumbled
- Two large hard-boiled eggs, sliced

INSTRUCTIONS

3. In a small bowl, combine the first five ingredients; mix well. Cover and refrigerate until serving. Place salad greens in a large bowl. Sprinkle with tomatoes, chicken, and bacon; garnish with eggs. Drizzle with dressing.

Nutrition Per Serving: 281 calories,19g fat,112mg cholesterol,324mg sodium,5g carbohydrate,23g protein.

Bonus recipes

Crunchy Chocolate Coconut Curls

TIME TO PREPARE
5 minutes

COOK TIME
15 minutes

Serving
6 People

INGREDIENTS

- Four egg yolks.
- One cup of shredded coconut.
- One cup of dark chocolate chips (unsweetened).
- ¾ cup walnuts (chopped).
- ¼ cup of coconut oil.
- 3 tbsp swerve.
- 3 tbsp butter.

INSTRUCTIONS

1. Preheat the oven at 175 degrees.
2. In a large bowl, mix egg yolks, coconut oil, butter, and swerve. Gradually stir in the chocolate chips, coconut, and walnuts.
3. Line a baking tray with greaseproof paper.
4. Using a tablespoon, place spoonful by a spoonful of the mixture on the tray.
5. Bake for 15-20 minutes until golden brown.

Nutrition Per Serving: Fat: 15g, Carbohydrates: 2g, Protein: 3g, Calories: 133

Bonus recipes

Not your caveman's chili

TIME TO PREPARE
10 minutes

COOK TIME
30 minutes

Serving
4 People

INGREDIENTS

- 2 lbs. Stew meat
- 1 medium onion
- 1 medium green pepper
- 1 cup beef broth
- 1/3 cup tomato paste
- 2 tbsp. Soy sauce
- 2 tbsp. Olive oil
- 2 tbsp. + 1 tsp. Chili powder
- 1 1/2 tsp. Cumin
- 2 tsp. Red boat fish sauce
- 2 tsp. Minced garlic
- 2 tsp. Paprika
- 1 tsp. Oregano
- 1 tsp. Cayenne pepper
- 1 tsp. Worcestershire

INSTRUCTIONS

1. Cube half stew meat into small cubes, and process the other half in a food processor into ground beef.
2. Chop pepper and onion into small pieces.
3. Combine all spices together to make sauce.
4. Sauté cubed beef in a pan until browned, transfer to a slow cooker. Do the same with the ground beef.
5. Sauté vegetables in the remaining fat in the pan until onions are translucent.
6. Add everything to the slow cooker and mix together.
7. Simmer for 1/2 hours on high, then simmer for 20-30 minutes without the top.

Nutrition Per Serving: 398 calories, 17.8g fats, 5.3g net carbs, and 51.8g protein.

Bonus recipes

Keto snickerdoodle cookies

TIME TO PREPARE
10 minutes

COOK TIME
15 minutes

Serving
12 People

INGREDIENTS

- 2 cups almond flour
- 1/4 cup coconut oil
- 1/4 cup maple syrup
- 1 tbsp. Vanilla
- 1/4 tsp. Baking soda
- 2 tbsp. Cinnamon

INSTRUCTIONS

1. Preheat oven to 350f.
2. Mix together your almond flour, baking soda, and salt.
3. In a separate bowl, mix together coconut oil, homemade maple syrup, vanilla, and stevia.
4. Mix dry ingredients into wet ingredients until a dough is formed.
5. Mix together cinnamon and erythritol until a powder is formed.
6. Roll dough into balls, roll into cinnamon mixture, then set them on a silpat.
7. Use the underside of a mason jar to flatten the balls, greasing the bottom as needed.
8. Bake for 9-10 minutes, remove, and let cool.

Nutrition Per Serving: 132 calories, 12.4g fats, 2g net carbs, and 3.4g protein.

Bonus recipes

Low carb spice cakes

TIME TO PREPARE
10 minutes

COOK TIME
25 minutes

Serving
12 People

INGREDIENTS

Spice cakes

- 2 cups honeyville almond flour
- 3/4 cup erythritol
- 1/2 cup salted butter
- 5 tbsp. Water
- 4 large eggs
- 2 tsp. Baking powder
- 1 tsp. Vanilla extract
- 1/2 tsp. Cinnamon
- 1/2 tsp. Nutmeg
- 1/2 tsp. Allspice
- 1/2 tsp. Ginger
- 1/4 tsp. Ground clove

Cream cheese frosting

- 8 oz. Cream cheese
- 2 tbsp. Butter
- 3 tbsp. Erythritol
- 1 tsp. Vanilla extract
- 1/2 of lemon's zest

INSTRUCTIONS

1. Preheat your oven to 350f.
2. In a mixing bowl, add your butter and sweetener. Cream it together until smooth.
3. Add 2 of your eggs and continue mixing it until combined, then add and mix in your last 2 eggs.
4. Grind up your spices, then add all the dry ingredients to the batter. Mix until smooth.
5. Add your water to the batter and mix well, until it is creamy.
6. Spray your cupcake tray, fill it about 3/4 of the way up, and put them in the oven for 15 minutes.

7. While they're cooking, cream together your cream cheese, butter, sweetener, vanilla, and lemon zest for the frosting.
8. Remove your cupcakes from the oven, let them cool for 15 minutes, and then frost them.

Nutrition Per Serving: 283 calories, 27g fats, 3.3g carbs, and 7.3g protein.

With over 100 recipes contained herein, the whole idea here is to give you a boost in terms of the choice of food that you will get to enjoy beyond the 28day meal plan provided. Designed to give the beginner an easier time while starting the keto diet, you will find that the meal plan gradually introduces the recipes, in an easy to follow format for you to prepare keto friendly, delicious foods that will serve you well on this ketogenic weight loss journey. Once you have completed the meal plan, please feel free to mix and match the recipes here to create your very own meal plans! Always remember to keep the macronutrient numbers in mind and do not go overboard with the daily calorie intake. Eating too much can still pack on the pounds, whether you are on keto or not.